Stagecraft and Statecraft

LEXINGTON STUDIES IN
POLITICAL COMMUNICATION

Series Editor: Robert E. Denton, Jr., Virginia Tech

This series encourages focused work examining the role and function of communication in the realm of politics including campaigns and elections, media, and political institutions.

TITLES IN SERIES:

Stagecraft and Statecraft

Advance and Media Events in Political Communication

DAN SCHILL

LEXINGTON BOOKS

A division of
ROWMAN & LITTLEFIELD PUBLISHERS, INC.
Lanham • Boulder • New York • Toronto • Plymouth, UK

LEXINGTON BOOKS

A division of Rowman & Littlefield Publishers, Inc.
A wholly owned subsidiary of The Rowman & Littlefield Publishing Group, Inc.
4501 Forbes Boulevard, Suite 200
Lanham, MD 20706

Estover Road
Plymouth PL6 7PY
United Kingdom

British Library Cataloguing in Publication Information Available

Library of Congress Cataloging-in-Publication Data

Schill, Dan, 1979–
   Stagecraft and statecraft : advance and media events in political communication /
Dan Schill.
      p. cm. — (Lexington studies in political communication)
   Includes bibliographical references and index.
   ISBN 978-0-7391-2861-9 (cloth : alk. paper) — ISBN 978-0-7391-2862-6 (pbk. :
alk. paper) — ISBN 978-0-7391-3700-0 (electronic)
   1. Mass media—Political aspects. 2. Communication planning. 3. Mass media—
Social aspects. I. Title.
   P95.8.S35 2009
   302.23—dc22   2008056105

Printed in the United States of America

⊚™ The paper used in this publication meets the minimum requirements of American
National Standard for Information Sciences—Permanence of Paper for Printed Library
Materials, ANSI/NISO Z39.48-1992.

Contents

Introduction

It was the perfect media event. In early 2003, President George W. Bush donned a flight suited labeled, "Commander-in-Chief," and took to the cockpit of a Navy jet to dramatically land on the homeward bound USS *Abraham Lincoln* aircraft carrier returning from the war in Iraq. In the made-for-television speech that followed, cheering soldiers surrounded Bush as he spoke from the carrier's flight deck—creating a powerful image of a triumphant military leader supported by his soldiers in a time of war. Using stagecraft techniques pioneered by previous administrations and perfected in the first three years of the Bush presidency, every element of the event was carefully controlled to create the most favorable pictures and headlines in the ensuing media coverage: the ship was positioned so the majestic Pacific Ocean would be the backdrop instead of the nearby California coast, the route of the ship was adjusted to steady the deck for the media cameras, a large banner reading "Mission Accomplished" was hung from the carrier's superstructure to reinforce the message of the event, and soldiers and jets were carefully arranged on the deck around the podium to frame the president.[1] The stagecraft did not end there—the Bush team overtook the ship and converted the military vessel into a television studio. Instead of the standard helicopter landing, Bush made a dramatic tailhook landing in a Viking S-3B, with the words "George W. Bush, commander-in-chief" painted under the cockpit window for the event.[2] Like a director giving instructions to Hollywood extras during a shoot, loudspeakers instructed sailors to hold off their applause until Bush officially exited the plane, and that "At that time, you'll be allowed to cheer as loudly as possible, and you'll be encouraged to show your affection."[3] The crowd of sailors and marines cheered as Bush announced: "my fellow Americans, major combat operations in Iraq have ended. In the battle of Iraq, the United States and our allies have prevailed."

These elements were created by the Bush administration to communicate an image of the president as a strong, engaged, and popular commander in chief. Media critic Frank Rich compared the White House news management team to filmmaker Jerry Bruckheimer, producer of the film Pearl Harbor: "If there was a single aesthetic that dominated this rousing scene it was that of Jerry Bruckheimer. . . . Like Pearl Harbor, which turned its titled attack and its aftermath into a pretty and blood-free victory jig, the new White House production sweetened reality."[4] This rosy perspective was not limited to the visual stagecraft—the president's remarks aboard the ship also sweetened the political and military realities in Iraq. In the text of the speech, Bush ignored growing concerns about a growing insurgency in Iraq and a lack of evidence of weapons of mass destruction and announced the end of major combat operations. The most frequently reported sound bite from the speech was one in which Bush celebrated the Iraq War and connected it to the September 11 terrorist attacks and the larger war on terror: "The battle of Iraq is one victory in a war on terror that began on September the 11th, 2001, and still goes on." Reagan image-maker Michael Deaver, who had developed many of the techniques used by the Bush PR team, similarly argued that the event had a large visual impact, "This is a powerful, powerful visual, not only of Bush as commander in chief, but of his strength as a world leader."[5]

The mosaic of images created by the event dominated the evening and follow day's news coverage. A close analysis of the news coverage of the event reveals that media accounts were overwhelmingly positive and always accompanied by pictures of Bush surrounded by troops, in the cockpit of the plane, walking in his flight suit with his flight helmet, or speaking on deck.[6] Tom Shales's report in the Washington Post was indicative of the media's coverage:

> this was not just a speech but a patriotic spectacular, with the ship and its crew serving as crucial backdrops for Bush's remarks, something to cheer the viewing nation and to make Bush look dramatically commander-in-chiefly. . . . There were several eloquent turns of phrase in the address . . . but they were overwhelmed by the visual impact, pictures both vast and intimate—vast when a camera gave viewers a wide shot of the whole ship and intimate when Bush was in close-up delivering his remarks.[7]

The narrative that emerged from the news accounts was consistent and clear: a thankful, strong, and popular president relived his military days by daringly landing aboard an active navy ship.

The television coverage was inundated with a wall-to-wall montage of powerful images of the president's plane landing, the president greeting and congratulating the crew, and speaking from the deck. Each television and cable network had correspondents on deck to chronicle every aspect of the made-for-television event, scene by scene. ABC's Bob Woodruff led World News

Tonight with a live shot from aboard the ship, hailing Bush's "impressive" landing, describing the supportive crew who was happy to have him aboard, highlighting the minutia of Bush's visit to the aircraft carrier, and broadcasting extensive b-roll favoring the president. On the *CBS Evening News*, Cynthia Bowers told of the majesty of the landing live from the ship: "From stem to stern, all eyes scanned the heavens, straining to be the first to pick out that flash of silver in overcast skies, because out of the thousands of landings this crew has seen, this one could be called historic." On the cable news channels, the response was familiar—enormous resources were poured into the coverage as the networks built up the landing for hours and continued running the ensuing pictures for days afterward. All spent most of their news time discussing the ins and outs of a carrier landing, Bush's history as a national guard pilot, and the early success in the military conflict—all synched to images of a triumphant Bush. For example, *Roll Call's* Mort Kondracke applauded the event on Fox News: "The only thing that could possibly exceed it is fictional, that was Bill Pullman in that wonderful movie, *Independence Day.* You know where he flies off and defeats the aliens. . . . But never mind that, this was fantastic theatre." Chris Matthews on MSNBC gave Bush a rave review: "spectacular speech, and I think what you saw there was a president with probably the closest identification I've seen since JFK of a commander-in-chief with the troops. I mean, he is one of them. I mean, he proved that tonight coming in, in uniform, coming aboard on an F-18, a fighter pilot—almost a fighter pilot—a former one—looking very much like a current one, a commander-in-chief in the flesh in uniform with the troops." While CNN propitiously showed hour after hour of images favorable to Bush, correspondent Frank Buckley said, "the headlines in the newspapers tomorrow morning will likely quote from the president's speech tonight. But it may be the pictures of the president that everyone will be talking about." The television networks, both broadcast and cable, covered the event with little regard to its framing and accepted the event at face value as staged by Bush's communication and advance staff.

The following day's newspaper coverage similarly affirmed Bush's media event and prominently featured multiple favorable images of the president. For example, the *Seattle Times* featured an account of how grateful the troops were for Bush's visit to the carrier:

> Behind them were nearly 10 months at sea, a journey of more than
> 100,000 miles and service during wartime. Ahead of them was home.
> But what mattered most yesterday for the crew of the Everett-based
> carrier USS *Abraham Lincoln* was a personally delivered word of
> thanks from the commander-in-chief.[8]

The *San Francisco Chronicle* printed five pictures of Bush on the carrier and said the event "allowed the president a picturesque—and powerful—opportunity to express the nation's gratitude to the troops in the glow of sunset while the *Lincoln* plowed toward San Diego after more than nine months at sea."[9] Newspaper after newspaper favorably described the event and Bush's stagecraft: the *New York Post*: "With his helmet tucked under his left arm and a wide grin on his face, Bush slapped backs, shook hands and posed for photos with the pilots, officers and on-deck sailors. . . . Many of them, already excited about the idea of finally reaching home today after 10 months at sea, seemed thrilled about the president's visit—and especially the way he arrived;"[10] the *New York Times*: "Earlier in the day, in a visit to the carrier that the White House arranged for maximum political effect, it was hard to tell Mr. Bush from the troops he was visiting;"[11] the *New York Daily News*: "The President emerged wearing a bulky flight suit and a broad grin, a helmet tucked under his arm. He strutted across the deck, snapping salutes at the excited pilots and sailors gathering around him."[12]

Editorials and columns were also overwhelmingly supportive of Bush's media event. The *Cleveland Plain Dealer* said the event offered "a glimpse of genuine affection between the commander and commanded, an expression of mutual admiration and gratitude as open as the sea through which the massive carrier steamed."[13] An editorial in the Riverside, California, *Press Enterprise*, strongly supported Bush's media event as "a memorable salute to all American troops for a self-sacrificing job well done" and argued that the viewpoint that criticized the event as a political ploy "belittles what Americans, and particularly their military, have just been through."[14] A similar column in the *Chicago Sun Times* by Neil Steinberg defended Bush's carrier landing as a fun diversion from negative news: "When I saw the president take off his helmet, smile broadly and greet the assembled servicemen and women, I thought: That looks like fun."[15] There were a few token commentators who criticized the event. The *Madison Capital Times* wrote that the troops "merit much more honor than to be cast in cameo roles as part of Karl Rove's propaganda machine,"[16] while James Werrell of the the *Herald* in Rock Hill, South Carolina, argued that the landing and subsequent speech were a phony public relations spectacle designed to obscure Bush's lackluster military career.[17]

The event was apparently so exciting that many reporters got caught up in the event's narrative and erroneously reported that the landing was groundbreaking and the first of its kind. For example, in an ostensible rush to praise the event, the *New York Times'* David Sanger made several obvious factual errors. Sanger wrote, "Never before has a president landed aboard a carrier at sea, much less taken controls on the aircraft. His decision to sleep aboard the ship this evening in the captain's quarters conjured images of the presidency at sea not seen since Franklin D. Roosevelt."[18] In fact, several presidents have landed aboard a carrier at sea and John Kennedy spent the night aboard the *Kitty Hawk*, which the *Times* corrected the following day.

The news media conformed to the message as it had been designed for publicity purposes; the dramatic images featured in their coverage and their reporting suggest they were more than willing participants in perpetuating the spectacle. The stories were nearly identical as if the reporters were working off the same script—the exact frame suggested by administration communication officials. Journalists praised the event in their coverage with comments such as: "the greatest photo-op of all time," "the mother of all photo opportunities," and "the kind of attention that other politicians can only dream about."[19] *PR Week* summarized the coverage: "The media couldn't seem to get enough of the images of the president on the flight deck, dressed in full aviator's garb, with his helmet under one arm. The images of a victorious and popular leader celebrating the liberation of a country from tyranny amid a backdrop of American power was universally hailed as dramatic and brilliantly choreographed."[20] In the coverage, the complicated military events in Iraq were reduced to bold headlines and eye-catching video, of course, as Sheldon Rampton and John Stauber, from the Center for Media and Democracy, describe: "the situation is more complicated than the images of victory that looked so unambiguously inspiring on American television."[21]

The event featured all of the elements journalists look for in a compelling story—drama, striking images, a personal glimpse of the president, emotion, patriotism, and impact. Most news accounts did not put the staged event in context nor report the behind the scenes stage management that created the event. Some reports did indicate that the event was a public relations attempt designed to bolster the president's image as a strong leader, however, they ignored facts that questioned the legitimacy of the landing. For example, they did not mention that Scott Sforza, a former ABC producer who worked as an advance man for Bush, spent several days on the carrier setting up and carefully choreographing every element of the event.[22] Other missing details include: the reunion of sailors and their families, who had been separated for 10 months, was delayed for an extra day so the carrier could be used as Bush's stage; a distance that would normally take 1 hour took 15 hours as the ship made lazy circles to accommodate the president; the White House initially said the ship was out of reach from traditional helicopters although the media and Bush's staff easily made the 30 minute trip by helicopter; the speech was timed to receive primetime television coverage and the dusk light favored by television producers; and the ship was slowed and turned whenever land became visible on the horizon to give the appearance that the ship was still hundreds of miles out at sea.[23] Further, journalists made comparisons to Bush's own military record without mentioning criticisms of his service and they did not question the event's connection to September 11 or al Qaeda—an implied and explicit claim advanced by the president. When stories were critical, the references were brief and overwhelmed by the drama of the pictures.

Perhaps as a result of the extensive positive media coverage, public opinion surveys from the time indicated that the American public supported the administration's staged event aboard the USS *Abraham Lincoln*. A *CBS News/New York Times* poll taken after the event found that 59 percent of Americans polled said the event was appropriate and not for Bush's own political gain.[24] Months after the event, Americans held similar views—a second poll taken at the end of the year by CNN, Gallup, and the *USA Today* in December, 2003, found that 57 percent of those surveyed said Bush's trip to the aircraft carrier was a good idea, and most said it was an effort to show support for the troops, not for political gain.

The Bush Administration's Event-Driven Approach

Bush's media event aboard the USS *Abraham Lincoln* was only one part of the Bush administration's news management during the Iraq War and throughout his presidency. The Top Gun moment was the culmination of a campaign to shape Bush's image in the minds of Americans that began in the 2000 campaign and that the White House communication staff planned to rely on in the 2004 campaign and beyond. The Bush administration used proven political marketing tools, such as video news releases, strategic polls, and leaks to influence public opinion; however, the dominant communication tool for the Bush administration was the media event.

The administration's news management approach was structured to remove power from the press, especially the Washington press corps, and force the news media to act as a conduit for their official message by only giving them stories via scripted events. Bush focused on holding controlled media events and "going public" to generate favorable pictures of the president and his policies instead of briefing and informing reporters. You can see this emphasis in his staff—a majority of Bush's communications staff were event planners, speech writers, and media affairs specialists.[25] Bush traveled around the country making campaign-type stops and reaching out to local and regional media, who are less likely to be critical in their coverage. In fact, Bush held more public events than any other previous president. As political communication scholar W. Lance Bennett observed, "The George W. Bush administration shifted its press strategy to an event-based news making program that often left the press on the sidelines to transmit well-controlled dramatic images to their audiences."[26]

Under this approach, the visual messages generated from each event were the primary focus of Bush communication staffers. The administration did not attempt to conceal the importance of visual images in their approach as Dan Bartlett,

President Bush's communications director, made clear in an interview with the *New York Times*: "We pay particular attention to not only what the president says but what the American people see. American's are leading busy lives, and sometimes they don't have the opportunity to read a story or listen to an entire broadcast. But if they can have an instant understanding of what the president is talking about by seeing 60 seconds of television, you can accomplish your goals as communicators."[27] The method was straightforward: carefully stage media events that would generate favorable images and headlines that the press could not ignore.

Bush used this approach throughout his presidency to push his policies, both domestic and international, including the war on terrorism, military spending, education, social security, and the environment, among others. For example, to promote his defense appropriations, Bush gave a speech in support of higher military spending to a friendly crowd at Eglin Air Force Base in Florida. This event resulted in at least eighty-six television stories in seven Florida broadcast markets and countless other print and radio stories.[28] From February to July 2005, Bush traveled to twenty-eight carefully selected states and held over fifty "conversations" with citizens to push his Social Security reforms.

The media event tactic was also a critical component of selling the war in Iraq to domestic and international audiences. Bush held hundreds of security themed events after the September 11 attacks and in the buildup to the war in Iraq. Nearly all of Bush's public appearances leading up to the Iraq War had a security theme—he gave a speech atop an Abrams tank in Ohio, he met with prisoners of war in Texas, and even gave a military theme to the White House Easter egg roll—when children of service men and women were the official guests.[29] During one tough stretch during the Iraq War, Bush made a surprise visit to Iraq that was widely covered in the press to share Thanksgiving with the troops—even though the turkey in the photos was plastic. The administration spent $250,000 on a television set at the United States Central Command forward headquarters in Doha, Qatar, so that official statements would be reported with polish and credibility. In Iraq, the toppling of a large statue of Saddam Hussein was stage-managed by U.S. Marines and one of the Army's psychological operation units adjacent to the Palestine Hotel which housed international media, complete with the psychological team using loudspeakers to encourage Iraqi citizens to assist the U.S. military in removing the statue.[30] This iconic moment that was widely assumed to be a spontaneous, Iraqi-civilian-led demonstration and proof of Iraqi support for the coalition military action was in reality a staged media event.

Just as the media accepted the Bush administration frame in the aircraft carrier landing and speech, the media typically covered these media events without questioning their public relations intent or legitimacy. This was especially clear in media coverage during the buildup to the invasion of Iraq. "The level of mediated public deliberation [in coverage of the second Iraq War] was so diminished as to make the preponderance of journalism little more than an in-strumental extension—a sort of propaganda helper—of the strategic goals of the administration," wrote political communication scholar W. Lance Ben-nett.[31] As the Bush administration made the case to the American people for preemptive war with Iraq, studies of the media coverage have found near per-fect journalistic participation with the Bush administrations frames on these is-sues even though contradictory information was available.[32] Susan Moeller's ex-tensive examination of media coverage on the weapons of mass destruction (WMD) issue found that news coverage gave greater weight to administration perspectives and discounted alternative perspectives, concluding that "many stories stenographically reported the incumbent administration's perspective on WMD, giving too little critical examination of the way officials framed the events, issues, threats, and policy options."[33]

The Bush administration has been stunningly successful in their use of po-litical marketing techniques to gather positive media coverage and win argu-ments in the public sphere. They fed the media beast, and the American people, a storyline most Americans wanted to hear and that fulfilled a post-9/11 hun-gering for a military show of force. Administration communication officials gave the country a compelling script, complete with a swaggering hero, a defined en-emy, maximum drama, and, of course, powerful pictures. The Bush administra-tion controlled the news images and this was an important factor in increasing public support for the war and for Bush's ability to effectively lead. Former *NBC News* producer and media commentator Alexandra Pelosi summarized the prob-lem by looking at how the administration used embedded reporters to their ad-vantage:

> As we witnessed when the Bush administration got their war on, they knew the only way to win in the court of public opinion was to get the media on board. So they invited all the ambitious young wannabe Scud studs to join in on the fun. Like dogs on the administration's leash, everyone jumped into their flak jackets and ran toward the bat-tlefield excited about the prospect of covering a war. It seemed like the only debate they had at the networks was who will be on the first float. On cue from the Pentagon, they named their coverage Opera-tion Iraqi Freedom. How would it be any different if we had a state-owned media?[34]

The administration, using time-tested news management techniques such as the media event, was able to write the script and stage the images that would appear on television, the Internet, and in print.

The news media failed in their public sphere role of informing the public and presenting multiple viewpoints in the marketplace of ideas and this failure had a direct affect on public opinion. Both before and after the war, a majority or near majority of Americans incorrectly believed that evidence existed of a link between Iraq and al Qaeda, the group who committed the 9/11 attacks, a claim which had been widely regarded as fallacious by the intelligence community. In the January before the war, 68 percent of Americans believed that Iraq played an important role in September 11, and in September that number remained at 49 percent.[35] Similarly, 22 percent believed that clear evidence of WMDs had been found in Iraq while 22 percent said that Hussein had used WMDs against American troops in the conflict. Months after Bush's aircraft carrier landing, 60 percent of Americans held at least one key misconception about Iraq's connection to al Qaeda, WMDs in the country, or world opinion of the war. Importantly, the number of misperceptions varied depending on the respondent's primary source of information about the war. Fox viewers (45 percent) had the highest percentage of misperceptions, while NPR/PBS had the lowest percentage of misperceptions (11 percent). In the middle were CBS (38 percent), CNN (31 percent), ABC (30 percent), NBC (30 percent), and the print media (25 percent).

Media Events and Advance in Political Communication

This case study of the Bush administration's news management and media event strategy is just one example of the power of news management and the role of media events in modern political communication. Newsmakers of every political stripe and every level of office use such events to attempt to build their image and gain favorable coverage from the press. While such photo-ops, publicity stunts, and pseudo-events have a long history and tradition in American politics, the tactic has been perfected in recent years and the current media environment increases its importance—political campaigns and governing now take place in a mass mediated democracy influenced largely by how well newsmakers stage events for media and public consumption. Media events are an important area of inquiry for several reasons. First, media events are significant because they have an agenda-setting function and can drive news coverage.[36] The day-to-day national political news cycle is frequently driven by media events—coverage of the president's appearances and the events of other important newsmakers. Because of this, media events have large audiences, which is a second reason scholars need to examine them. Most events have considerable direct audiences, and are also given national audiences via the mass media and news coverage.[37] In presidential elections, research has found that events are held in areas with large and diverse populations and that most eligible voters live in geographic areas that receive at least one visit by a presidential candidate.[38] Third, media events are a critical strategy used by politicians and political organizations to construct their political image.[39] Since the introduction of television, political candidates and elected officials have often relied on media events for image making and candidate appearances are increasing both in number and in geographic scope over time.[40] Finally, not only are we campaigning by media event—we are also now governing via media event. In effect, we debate and deliberate through media events.

Despite their importance in modern public affairs, scholars have a limited understanding of how these events are constructed, covered by the news media, and received by voters. Further, there is a paucity of research examining the functions and effects of media events, and no systematic method for analyzing media events. Political communication scholars often mention media events and claim they are important without detailed analyses of those events.[41] The limited research on events either compares mediated versions of events to their nonmediated counterparts,[42] criticizes the nominating conventions as pseudo-events,[43] or applies a basic pseudo-event framework to news coverage.[44] It is essential to understand media events because they influence the media agenda, media frames, and ultimately, each individual's mass mediated reality. There is a vital need for an in-depth examination of media events and their impact on the public sphere. In addressing this need, this book is an exploration of the modern media event and its role in political communication—how events are created, managed, covered, and received.

This book focuses on a few "big" questions regarding how candidates and elected officials stage media events and to what extent those events influence media coverage and voter opinions of newsmakers—how political stagecraft influences statecraft. To address these questions, I follow a methodology advocated by King, Koehane, and Verba,[45] Shaw,[46] and Yin[47]: I begin with broad research questions about how media events function and are constructed to establish theoretical sensitivity; I then identify and describe this phenomenon and its constituent parts, followed by an analysis of its occurrences and effects. This perspective is "one part definitional, one part descriptive, and one part analytic."[48] The primary source of data is historical documents from the archives at Presidential Libraries for presidents John F. Kennedy, Lyndon B. Johnson, Richard Nixon, Gerald R. Ford, Jimmy Carter, Ronald Reagan, and George H. W. Bush. At each of these libraries, all available documents related to media events, advance offices and efforts, press offices, and communication offices were selected for analysis. The majority of these documents came from the White House Staff and Office Files collections, which consist of individual folders from White House offices and specific staff members. These documents included the Advance Operations Manuals from each president, strategy memos pertaining to media events, communication strategy and press management documents, detailed schedules of the president, event-planning documents, speechwriting drafts and documents related to the speeches from the events, and handwritten notes by the communications staff. Additionally, unedited video of various aspects of each event and still images of each event, including multiple shots from media areas, were examined where available in the archives as taken by White House photographers and videographers. Analysis of these historical documents was corroborated with three additional data sources: interviews with advance men and women, media accounts of presidential events, and case study analyses of media events and advance in the 2008 presidential primaries and general election. Interviews with Democratic and Republican advance staff were conducted to ascertain their understanding of advance and events and autobiographies and memoirs of advance men and women were consulted for verification. Media coverage from CBS, ABC, and NBC for key events was acquired from the Vanderbilt Television Archive and newspaper stories from electronic databases. Finally, the 2008 presidential election was used as an extended case study to test conclusions that emerged from the historical documents in a contemporary context. Television news coverage from three major networks and three cable networks was recorded and comprehensively analyzed from April 29, 2007 to June 10, 2008 for the primary and from June 11, 2008 to November 4, 2008 for the general election. In addition to the primary texts, secondary sources were used as a supplement to fill in the gaps where the primary sources were lacking.

Plan of the Book

The book begins with an introduction of the role of candidates and the media in constructing candidate images and the current state of our mass-mediated democracy in the first chapter. This first chapter includes a review of the major theories of media effects such as agenda setting and framing and a brief discussion of the role of visual images in politics and how voters process political messages. The second chapter focuses on media events—how and why candidates stage events, the types of events, the role of journalists in covering media events, and the strategies media event planners use to improve the success of their event. The third chapter more specifically examines the advance consultants who create, visually write, and manage these events. This chapter explains the multiple job responsibilities of advance men and women and includes a detailed explanation of the specific tactics in the advance staffer's toolbox such as crowd building, using signs and banners, and relying on patriotic symbols. In the fourth chapter, the book considers why media events exert such power on our political debate and the rhetorical impact of media events on voters and the press. The book concludes in the fifth and final chapter, which evaluates the implications, both positive and negative, of media events in American political affairs and suggests future areas of interest for journalists, citizens, and scholars.

Notes

1. Scott Lindlaw, "Accommodating TV-Friendly Presidential Visit Caused a Few Changes in Navy Carrier's Routine," *Associated Press* (May 2, 2003).

2. Bill Kaczor, "Bush's 'Navy One' Makes Final Flight," *Tallahassee Democrat* (July 16, 2003).

3. Karen DeYoung, "Bush Proclaims Victory in Iraq: Work on Terror is Ongoing, President Says," *Washington Post* (May 2, 2003), A1.

4. Frank Rich, *The Greatest Story Ever Sold: The Decline and Fall of Truth from 9/11 to Katrina* (New York: Penguin, 2006), 90–91.

5. Dana Milbank, "The Military is the Message: Triumphant President Casts Strong Image for '04 Election," *Washington Post* (May 2, 2003), A24.

6. Footage was recorded on computer, television quotes from electronic transcripts.

7. Tom Shales, "Aboard the *Lincoln*: A White House Spectacular," *Washington Post* (May 2, 2004), C1.

8. Rachel Tuinstra, "A Moment of Thanks after 10 Months at Sea," *Seattle Times* (May 2, 2003), A1.

9. Carla Marinucci, "Bush Thanks Troops: 'The Tyrant Has Fallen,' President Addresses Nation from Aircraft Carrier Returning from War," *San Francisco Chronicle* (May 2, 2003), A1.

10. Brian Blomquist, "Sky Chief Bush Hits the Deck—Pilots War Jet en Route to Carrier," *New York Post* (May 2, 2003), 2.

11. David E. Sanger, "Bush Declares 'One Victory in War on Terror,'" *New York Times* (May 2, 2003), 1.

12. Helen Kennedy, "Bush Swoops in, Lands on Carrier, Calls Liberation of Iraq Blow against Terrorism," *New York Daily News* (May 2, 2003), 2.

13. *Plain Dealer*, "The War on Terrorism: Amid the Exultation over a Victory Well Won, Bush Levels with the Troops and the Nation: More Battles Await," *Plain Dealer* (Cleveland, OH) (May 3, 2003), B8.

14. *Press-Enterprise*, "Editorials: Our View," *Press Enterprise* (Riverside, CA) (May 3, 2003), A10.

15. Neil Steinberg, "Cool Speech Site Shows Bush Knows How to Have Fun," *Chicago Sun-Times* (May 2, 2003), 24.

16. *Capital Times*, "Rove Exploits the Military," *Capital Times* (Madison, WI) (May 3, 2003), 10A.

17. James Werrell, "Was This Photo Op Really Necessary?" *Herald* (Rock Hill, SC) (May 9, 2003), 6A.

18. David E. Sanger, "In Full Flight Regalia, the President Enjoys a 'Top Gun' Moment," *New York Times* (May 2, 2003), 17.

19. Hugh Clifton, "President's Aircraft-Carrier Appearance Hailed as Brilliant PR," *PR Week* (May 19, 2003).

20. Hugh Clifton, "President's Aircraft-Carrier," para 1.

21. Sheldon Rampton and John Stauber, *Weapons of Mass Deception: The Uses of Propaganda in Bush's War on Iraq* (New York: Tarcher/Penguin, 2003), 7.

22. Elizabeth Bumiller, "Keepers of Bush Image Lift Stagecraft to New Heights," *New York Times* (May 16, 2003), 1.

23. See Bumiller, "Keepers of Bush," 1; and Werrell, "Was This Photo Op," 6A.

24. *National Journal Poll Track*, "2003 Polling." Retrieved December 20, 2005, from http://nationaljournal.com/members/polltrack/2003.

25. Ryan Lizza, "The White House Doesn't Need the Press," *New York Times* (December 9, 2001), 108.

26. W. Lance Bennett, *News: The Politics of Illusion* (6th ed.) (New York: Pearson/Longman, 2005), 140.

27. Cited in Bumiller, "Keepers of Bush," 1.

28. Elizabeth Bumiller, "Presidential Travel: It's All about Local News," *New York Times* (February 11, 2002), 24.

29. Diego Ibarguen, "Powerful Images in Landing on Carrier; Unprecedented Arrival via Jet Helps Bathe Bush in Military's Aura," *Times Union* (Albany, NY) (May 2, 2003), A6.

30. Gregory Fontenot, E. J. Degen, and David Tohn, *On Point: The United States Army in Operation Iraqi Freedom* (Annapolis, MD: Naval Institute Press, 2005), 336–38.

31. W. Lance Bennett, "Operation Perfect Storm: The Press and the Iraq War," *Political Communication Report* 13(3) (2003): 1.

32. See Bennett, *News*; and Susan D. Moeller, "Media Coverage of Weapons of Mass Destruction," (March 4, 2004). Retrieved December 7, 2005, from Center for International and Security Studies at Maryland: http://www.cissm.umd.edu/documents/WMD-study_short.pdf

33. Moeller, "Media Coverage," 3.

34. Alexandra Pelosi, *Sneaking into the Flying Circus: How the Media Turn our Presidential Campaigns into Freak Shows* (New York: Free Press, 2005), xiii.

35. Steven Kull, Clay Ramsay, and Evan Lewis, "Misperceptions, the Media, and the Iraq War," *Political Science Quarterly* 118(4) (2003): 569–98.

36. Samuel Kernell, *Going Public: New Strategies of Presidential Leadership* (3rd ed.) (Washington, DC: CQ Press, 1997).

37. Scott L. Althaus, Peter F. Nardulli, and Daron R. Shaw, "Candidate Appearances in Presidential Elections, 1972–2000," *Political Communication* 19 (2002): 49–72; Daron R. Shaw, *The Race to 270: The Electoral College and the Campaign Strategies of 2000 and 2004* (Chicago, IL: University of Chicago Press, 2006); Kathleen Hall Jamieson and Karlyn Kohrs Campbell, *The Interplay of Influence: News, Advertising, Politics, and the Internet* (Belmont, CA: Wadsworth, 2005).

38. Althaus, Nardulli, and Shaw, "Candidate Appearances," 49–72.

39. Bennett, *News*; and Robert Schmuhl, *Statecraft and Stagecraft: American Political Life in the Age of Personality* (Notre Dame, IN: University of Notre Dame Press, 1990).

40. Althaus, Nardulli, and Shaw, "Candidate Appearances," 49–72.

41. Bennett, *News*; Kernell, *Going Public*; and Schmuhl, *Stagecraft*.

42. For example, Lynda Lee Kaid, Craig Corgan, and Phil Clampitt, "Perceptions of a Political Campaign Event: Media vs. Personal Viewing," *Journal of Broadcasting* 30 (1976): 303–12; and G. E. Lang and K. Lang. "The Unique Perspective of Television and Its Effects: A Pilot Study," *American Sociological Review* 18 (1953): 3–12.

43. For example. John M. Arwood, "Televised Political Conventions as Pseudo-Events: Proposals for More Substantive Campaign Coverage in 1992," *University of Missouri-Columbia*.

44. For example, W. Lance Bennett, "Beyond Pseudoevents: Election News as Reality TV," *American Behavioral Scientist* 49 (2005): 364–78.

45. Gary King, Robert O. Keohane, and Sidney Verba. *Designing Social Inquiry: Scientific Inference in Qualitative Research* (Princeton, NJ: Princeton Press, 1994).

46. Shaw, *The Race to 270*.

47. Robert K. Yin, *Case Study Research: Design and Methods* (Thousand Oaks, CA: Sage, 2002).

48. Shaw, *The Race to 270*, 9.

CHAPTER 1

Mass-Mediated Politics and Constructed Candidates

Effective political leaders appreciate that most Americans understand politics through the mass media—that political knowledge is mediated and socially constructed. Most American's do not have the ability to shake hands with their president, investigate policy proposals, or directly hear the president defend his policies; however, Americans still have strong attitudes and beliefs of politicians and policies, developed at least in part from their exposure to images and messages presented in the news. In Walter Lippmann's terms, the "pictures in our head" of our leaders are created through an individual's contact with the media instead of direct experience.[1] The purpose of this chapter is to provide a theoretical foundation upon which to discuss the role of media events in American political communication through a brief review of (1) media effects theory, (2) news management strategies and tactics, (3) the impact of visual symbols in politics, and (4) previous research on political information processing.

For most Americans, political affairs come into their homes via television, radio, print, and increasingly, the Internet. As such, politics, campaigns, and candidates are constructed in the mass media.[2] This construction has a tremendous impact on political campaigns and the political process in general. Individuals pick and chose among the information presented to them by the media, filtering these messages through their own perceptual screens and discussing the issues with others.[3] Through this process, political knowledge, images, and attitudes work together to create an individual's "mass-mediated reality."[4]

Political communication scholars have long recognized that political knowledge is mediated.[5] Such scholars have grounded their work in the various theoretical approaches. For example, George Herbert Mead and other symbolic interaction theorists argued that the individual mind and self arise out of social processes.[6] Similarly, Kenneth Burke's dramatism theory posits that all human beings are symbol-using actors and that life itself is theater.[7] Individuals, Burke argued, bring to their rhetorical interactions a set of ideologies or frames that are derived from the social world. These perspectives and others[8] have been integrated under the umbrella of social construction of reality theory.

The theoretical position that unites all social constructionists is that reality is shaped through the social process of communication—what a person knows and thinks is created through social interaction, and each individual has their own subjective reality. "Social constructionism is principally concerned with elucidating the process by which people come to describe, explain, or otherwise account for the world in which they live," summarized Gergen.[9] Since communication is the primary interaction tool, social constructionists analyze the verbal and nonverbal symbols that work to constitute our realities. Cromby and Nightingale reviewed the centrality of language in shaping knowledge: "It is the social reproduction and transformation of structures of meaning, conventions, morals, and discursive practices that principally constitutes our relationships and ourselves. This implies that language, both as the dominant carrier of categories and meanings and as the medium which provides much of the raw material for our activity, is central."[10] Nimmo and Combs, scholars who initially applied a social constructionist perspective to political communication, offer their theoretical assumptions based on this model: "(1) our everyday, taken-for-granted reality is a delusion; (2) reality is created, constructed, through communication, not expressed by it; (3) for any situation there is no single reality, no one objective truth, but multiple subjectively derived realities."[11]

While not necessarily supporting the more extreme of Nimmo and Combs's positions, modern political communication, media, and public opinion scholars generally share their approach. Instead of examining social interaction; the emphasis of these scholars is on mediated interactions. By their nature, media are not absolute reflections of reality, and are instead manipulations.[12] The reality of an event for a television viewer is always different from the reality experienced by an event's participants—the normal news selection and editing techniques skew reality. The classic study demonstrating this effect is Kurt and Gladys Lang's analysis of a 1951 parade honoring General Douglas MacArthur in Chicago.[13] The Langs compared observations from individuals who attended the parade in person to those who watched the parade on television. Direct observers of the parade found little enthusiasm and small crowds; television viewers, however, reported that the parade was an exciting and triumphant event. In a similar study, Kaid, Corgan, and Clampitt found that those who attended a speech in-person recalled more content from the speech and were more influenced by the speech than those who had got information about the event from the media.[14]

Television news has long been the dominant source of information for the majority of Americans. Despite the widespread use of the Internet for political information, television remains the most widely used source. On an average day,

57 percent of Americans watch television news, compared to 35 percent who listen to radio news, 34 percent who read a newspaper, and 29 percent who get their news online.[15] The average viewer watches 54 minutes of news daily and nearly half (48 percent) watch TV news for a half-hour or more per day. These relatively simple statistics disguise the complicated media and political landscape a contemporary citizen encounters. The sheer amount of information available and the profusion of media outlets have complicated the role of citizen. In addition to the nightly news on the three major networks; local news has expanded to at least two hours in most markets, news magazine programs now air regularly, and cable television provides at least four 24-hour all-news channels to viewers. Even with this proliferation of information sources, most Americans lack basic knowledge of major political issues,[16] although television news gives viewers the illusion of being informed.[17]

Agenda Setting, Priming, and Framing

Since most Americans are dependent on the news media for information on political affairs, it is necessary to examine what issues the media promotes and how those issues are covered. Agenda setting is the ongoing competition between the media, political professionals, and the public to set which issues will receive attention in the public sphere. Bernard Cohen argued that the press set the agenda for the public: "the press may not be successful much of the time telling people what to think, but it is stunningly successful in telling its readers what to think about. . . . The world will look different to different people, depending . . . on the map that is drawn for them by writers, editors, and publishers of the papers they read."[18] The first quantitative study of this agenda-setting function supported earlier anecdotal analyses and concluded that "the mass media sets the agenda for each political campaign, influencing the salience of attitudes toward political issues."[19] Extensive later analyses found that there is a strong positive correlation, and often a causal relationship, between the media agenda and the public agenda, especially on issues that do not directly affect the lives of the public, such as foreign policy.[20] Agenda setting is one of the most popular theories in political science and political communication and has been extended to virtually every arena of politics and public life, and is the most popular tool for explaining the interplay between the media, candidates, and voters in political campaigns.[21]

Since media attention has been found to be an important contributor in shaping public opinion, scholars are increasingly examining the factors that influence the media agenda, a body of research referred to as both media agenda setting[22] and agenda building.[23] This type of research includes studies of the various kinds of influences on media agendas, including public relations efforts, news sources, other media coverage, and the norms and conventions of journalism. For instance, agenda-building research has found that the single most influential news source in the United States is the president.[24] For example, one study observed that the agenda of fifteen issues in Richard Nixon's 1970 State of the Union address predicted the subsequent month's news coverage both in print and on television.[25] A similar study revealed that nearly half of the front-page news stories in the *New York Times* and the *Washington Post* from 1949 to 1969 were based on press releases, press conferences, media events, and other public relations efforts.[26] Over 70 percent of news coverage of the presidency during those years was the result of agenda-building efforts.[27] While there is some research on what factors set the media agenda,[28] there is a lack of contemporary, agenda-building research. Research that examines today's mass media is still needed to further develop a theoretical understanding of the complex relationship between the press and the newsmakers they cover.

Further, understanding what the media agenda is and how it is formed is critical because the media have a "priming effect" on viewers. "By calling attention to some matters while ignoring others, television news influences the standards by which governments, presidents, policies, and candidates for office are judged."[29] Priming theory argues that when people make political judgments about complex political phenomena, they are unable to consider all that they know and instead make judgments based on the bits and pieces of memory that are readily accessible. The news media play a determinate role in making information more accessible and by influencing the terms by which political judgments are reached and political choices made. Iyengar and Kinder describe this process in their initial book on the subject: "When primed by television news stories that focus on national defense, people judge the president largely by how well he has provided, as they see it, for the nation's defense; when primed by stories about inflation, people evaluate the president by how he managed, in their view, to keep prices down, and so on."[30]

Not only does the mass media play a priming role in making information accessible, media perspectives can also frame the issues for audiences. Framing is a general communication concept defined by framing authority Robert Entman as: "to select some aspects of a perceived reality and make them more salient in a communicating text, in such a way as to promote a particular problem definition, causal interpretation, moral evaluation, and/or treatment recommendation for the item described."[31] Framing is of critical importance in political communication because how an issue is framed may influence a person's reaction to that issue. In the political context, "framing is the process by which a communication source, such as a news organization [or political leader, public relations officer, political advertising consultant, or news consumer], defines and constructs a political issue or public controversy."[32] Yet, it is not completely clear how media frames and news narratives develop and change over time.[33]

To review, the news may not be a mirror image of political reality, yet it can have important effects on what issues are perceived as significant, how political decisions are made, how the public feels about its leaders, and which politicians and organizations are framed as credible and effective. These theories of agenda setting, agenda building, priming, and framing establish a theoretical foundation from which to analyze advance and media events. The communication professionals who stage events realize the powerful role the press plays in interpreting the candidates and attempt to use the media to their advantage through media events. This book examines the techniques that these advance men and women use to influence the news media—their attempts at agenda building—and the success of those efforts of framing the president and his policies.

News Management Model and Tactics

Based on their knowledge of the role the news media play in the political process, politicians and political groups attempt to manipulate the news agenda to receive recognition, achieve favorable coverage, and attack their political enemies. Influencing the news agenda and controlling political images in the news is the primary focus of political communication. Bennett explains: "The core of the strategic communication process involves developing and communicating a message that promotes the political goals of a campaign by appealing to a targeted audience and holding the symbolic high ground if it comes under attack."[34] According to Bennett, the message construction process is composed of four parts: (1) Composing a simple theme or message for the audience to use in thinking about the political issue; (2) Saturating communication channels with this message so that it will overpower competing messages; (3) Constructing a context of credibility for the message by finding a dramatic setting and recognized sources to deliver it, followed by endorsements from prominent supporters; and (4) Delivering the message with the right scripting (particularly sound bites) and post-delivery spin to lead journalists to pick the right category for accentuating the message. Each of these four elements can be accomplished with a well-designed public appearance.

Political communicators implement a wide array of communication strategies and political marketing techniques to manage the news. The modern president relies on these techniques not only to win elections, but to be a successful leader once in office.[35] The strategies are equally important in lower level races as well: congressional members are now in a permanent campaign, state and local officials now campaign with similar techniques, and federal and state agencies now have their own public relations divisions. Media scholar Schmuhl explains:

> Coached by communications consultants and guided by public opin-
> ion pollsters—conspicuous political participants since the post–1968
> reformation—candidates rely on ads, press conferences, photo op-
> portunities and a myriad other media-related events to deliver their
> messages. Smokeless politics makes the various modes of mass com-
> munication, especially television, central participants in the electoral
> process. It is largely through the media that we come to know and to
> judge public figures. A campaign becomes a political production that
> dramatizes and projects the candidate's personality as well as policies
> and proposals.[36]

These news management techniques include strategic symbol use, market research, press management, and the staging of media events.

At the most basic level, political communicators select symbols and words that are most favorable to their objective. Symbols play a central role in defin-
ing political situations. The symbol that is chosen to describe an issue can frame the debate around the issue and influence public attitudes toward that subject. For example, attitudes toward the estate tax dramatically shifted when opponents of the tax renamed it the death tax.[37] Similarly, the Defense Department has created a series of symbols designed to reinterpret the meaning of military actions, such as "collateral damage," "friendly fire," and "smart bombs."

Market research, such as polling, focus groups, and electronic dial response groups, is a critical element in a campaign's attempt to influence the news media and public opinion. For instance, polls are conducted at several moments in a campaign: benchmark polls inform decisions about whether or not to run; op-
position and trial heat polls expose the competitor's weaknesses; issue polls test various topics' traction among voters; and tracking polls monitor support for the candidate. In a focus group, likely voters discuss political issues and candidates while consultants monitor the discussion via videotape or a two-way mirror. In an electronic dial response group, participants indicate their opinion of a message second-by-second on a dial while viewing a political message. By providing data on the potential effects of persuasive appeals on various audiences, these re-
search tools inform the candidate's later communication decisions with the me-
dia and the public.

Press management is also a daily consideration of most political actors. Most newsmakers strive to maintain friendly relationships with the press and assist in their reporting of the news—they will schedule interviews and press conferences at convenient times, supply well-timed news releases, give off-the-record interviews, and coordinate food, travel, and lodging for the traveling press corp. The press and politician are inextricably intertwined: "There exists between the candidate and the media an accommodation which is, by and large, mutually beneficial: news organizations define elections as important events which must be covered; candidates use news reporting as the most inexpensive way to communicate to the public."[38] Politicians, government organizations, and other political groups provide news to the media, and are more likely to have their views reported as a result. Barber (1980) argues that "[Candidates] learn to use journalism, as journalism uses them. They and the candidates grapple in a reciprocal relationship of mutual exploitation, a political symbiosis. If the journalists are the new kingmakers, the candidates are the new storytellers, active plotters of dramas they hope will win for them."[39]

In summary, people learn about political affairs and their elected officials via the mass media, predominantly television. The news media often plays an agenda-setting role in telling people what issues are important and framing the debate surrounding those issues. Newsmakers have understood the central role the news media plays in defining issues and have developed a series of techniques that attempt to influence the media agenda and generate favorable coverage. One of the most common of these news management techniques is the media event. One reason media events are so influential is because of their focus on visual symbols. The next section reviews the literature regarding visual communication in political contexts, an area increasing in importance with the popularity of television as a campaign information source.

Visual Symbols in Political Communication

Television is by far the most important communication channel in modern political communication. The increasing impact of television in political campaigns is various and well documented. Television has decreased the importance of political parties,[40] focused attention on horse race coverage,[41] increased the importance of emotional appeals,[42] shifted campaign spending to television advertising,[43] and burgeoned the importance of visual symbols. Television is a visual medium at its core.[44] As more voters depend on television for political information, the importance of visual symbols increases. Doris Graber observed that television has "restored nonverbal symbols to a primacy previously enjoyed only in the preliterate age of human history."[45]

Candidates have perfected the art of the sound bite—speaking in brief, complete statements that are easily incorporated into media accounts and support the candidate's objectives. Candidates must communicate their information quickly and efficiently because the length of the sound bite has steadily decreased from 43 seconds in 1968 to 7.7 seconds in 2004.[46] While sound bites remain a critically important strategy, image bites, brief visual shots or video clips where candidates are shown but not heard, are quickly growing in importance.[47] In their study of network television news from the 1992, 1996, 2000, and 2004 American presidential campaign, Bucy and Grabe found that sound bites accounted for 14.3 percent of election coverage while image bites comprised 25.1 percent of coverage, with candidate-focused image bites averaging 25.8 seconds per story in 2004.[48]

This visual image-making by politicians is nothing new. American politicians have always attempted to control how their visual image is presented in the media.[49] Teddy Roosevelt took reporters on his hunting trips and hikes but wouldn't allow himself to be photographed playing tennis. John Kennedy carefully considered his appearance before debating Richard Nixon, and individuals who watched the first presidential debate in 1960 on television preferred the photogenic Kennedy, while those in the hall and listening via radio favored Nixon.[50] Ross Perot used several elaborate charts and graphs to analyze the economy and argue his candidacy in 1992, Lamar Alexander built his image by wearing a sturdy flannel shirt, and Al Gore attempted to reform his stiff image by wearing informal sweaters in the 2000 primary elections.[51] These memorable examples are just a few of the countless examples of how politicians have used visual communication to their advantage.

Visual symbols are the most dominant mode of learning[52] and neurologists have found that images play a central role in developing a sense of self and consciousness.[53] The language of pictures quickly and memorably communicates concepts to the audience in a fashion that they easily understand.[54] As Blair notes, "paintings and sculptures, and the visual component of movies, television programs and commercial and political advertising, are enormously powerful influences on attitudes and beliefs."[55] Experimental research examining photos in campaign direct mail has found that "a single photograph can have a clear impact on voters' judgments regarding a candidate's congressional demeanor, competence, leadership ability, attractiveness, likeableness, and integrity."[56] Audiences process visual symbols more quickly and efficiently than written texts and visual symbols contain more information than other symbol types.[57] Viewers remember the visuals presented in television news stories more easily than the verbal narration,[58] especially when those images lead to feelings of fear anger, or disgust.[59] Visuals are also more memorable and aid in information recall,[60] especially when the pictures contain dramatic information not known to the receiver.[61] One study by Kipper demonstrated that viewers also recall more information about a scene when the scene is filmed with a moving rather than a fixed camera.[62] Research has also found that people believe what they see more than what they hear or read[63] and that when the visual and verbal message are in conflict, viewers have difficulty remembering the verbal information[64] and the visual symbol usually trumps the verbal symbol.[65] All things being equal, research suggests that visual messages dominate other messages when presented simultaneously.[66]

Visual communication scholar Schweiger summarized the advantages visual images have over their linguistic counterparts: "Pictures tend to have a higher activating potential than texts. Imagery research has proved that pictures can be remembered better than words. Pictures are at the very least suitable as verbal stimuli to create a positive product image and to convince the consumer to buy. Attitudes and images can be changed without slogans."[67] Political rhetoric scholars Nelson and Doyton similarly asserted that "the persuasion (of political messages) is in the delivery, and the delivery is in the details," adding that "the delivery is in the memorable flavors, colors, images, movements, voices, musics, and characters."[68] The power of visual communication lies in its ability to transmit those flavors, colors, images, and movements to voters who use those details to form political opinions and make political judgments.

How Voters Process Political Information

We live busy lives in a world that is oversaturated with messages, including political messages. When an audience member sees coverage of a media event on television or in print, most people do not have the motivation or ability to process every political message critically and in an in-depth manner. Instead, individuals process most messages and evaluate political candidates based on peripheral cues or information shortcuts. Americans engage in practical thinking about government called "low-information rationality."[69] Voters do not possess a great deal of knowledge or information on the candidates or the issues, but instead have learned to use a series of mental shortcuts, also called heuristic or peripheral cues, to rationally make inferences about candidates, parties, and issues. These peripheral cues include endorsements of prominent figures, connections to political parties, and conversations with others to guide their decisions. Voters may also use "gut" feelings about their likes and dislikes to make political choices.[70] Another important type of peripheral cue voters use in low information rationality processing is visual and nonverbal symbols.[71]

The low information rationality processing theory is grounded in the Elaboration Likelihood Model. The Elaboration Likelihood Model is a process model of persuasion that examines how receivers cognitively respond to various persuasive messages.[72] This model posits that there are two routes persuasive messages can take when processed by receivers—labeled the central route and the peripheral route. When messages take the central route, receivers think and critically analyze the messages in a process labeled elaboration. Messages that take this route, when accepted by the receiver, are typically more long lasting and resistant in change. In order to be processed using this central route, receivers must have the motivation to listen to the message and the ability to process the message. The vast majorities of messages are not processed centrally and are instead processed in the second route to persuasion called the peripheral route. Instead of critically analyzing the arguments, messages taking this route are judged based on peripheral cues, such as source credibility. These messages can be effective, but are typically successful only when the peripheral cue remains cognitively present for the receivers. Media events are effective because they provide audiences with numerous peripheral cues from which audiences can interpret and understand an event. The symbols in an event are designed to be understood and processed quickly and easily.

Conclusion

We now live in "mass media democracy" in which voters learn about candidates largely via the sights and sounds broadcast into their homes by television. The news media plays an important role in framing the candidates and the issues, dictating which issues are important, and instructing voters to pay attention to certain aspects of the political debate while ignoring others. Candidates understand this centrality of the media in both campaigning and governing, and have developed a collection of news management techniques and hired communication consultants in an attempt to influence this coverage. The foremost among these strategies is the staged media event that is created by advance men and women to prompt favorable coverage and attention from voters. One reason for media events importance is their ability to create verbal sound bites and visual image bites which voters use as heuristics to form political opinions and make political decisions.

Notes

1. Walter Lippmann, *Public Opinion* (New York: Free Press, 1965).

2. W. Lance Bennett, *News: The Politics of Illusion*, 6th ed. (New York: Pearson/Longman, 2005); Girish J. Gulati, Marion R. Just, and Ann N. Crigler, "News Coverage of Political Campaigns," in *Handbook of Political Communication Research*, ed. Lynda Lee Kaid (Mahwah, N.J.: Lawrence Erlbaum, 2004), 237–56.

3. Karen S. Johnson-Cartee, *News Narratives and News Framing: Constructing Political Reality* (Lanham, MD: Rowman & Littlefield, 2005).

4. Dan D. Nimmo and James E. Combs, *Mediated Political Realities* (New York: Longman, 1983).

5. See, for example, Daniel J. Boorstin, *The Image: A Guide to Pseudo-Events in America* (New York: Harper & Row, 1964); Lippman, *Public Opinion*; Nimmo and Combs, *Mediated Political Realities.*

6. George Herbert Mead and Charles W. Morris, *Mind, Self, and Society: From the Standpoint of a Social Behaviorist* (Chicago: University of Chicago Press, 1967).

7. Kenneth Burke, *A Grammar of Motives* (New York: Prentice-Hall, 1945); Kenneth Burke, *A Rhetoric of Motives* (New York: Prentice-Hall, 1950).

8. For example, Herbert Blumer, *Symbolic Interactionism: Perspective and Method* (Englewood Cliffs, NJ: Prentice-Hall, 1969); Erving Goffman, *The Presentation of Self in Everyday Life* (Garden City, NY: Doubleday, 1959).

9. Kenneth J. Gergen, "Social Constructionist Inquiry: Context and Implications," in *The Social Construction of the Person*, ed. Kenneth J. Gergen and Keith E. Davis (New York: Springer-Verlag, 1985), 3–4.

10. John Cromby and David J. Nightingale, "What's Wrong with Social Constructionism?" in *Social Constructionist Psychology: A Critical Analysis of Theory and Practice*, ed. David J. Nightingale and John Cromby (Philadelphia: Open University Press, 1999), 4.

11. Nimmo and Combs, *Mediated Political Realities*, 3.

12. Anne Marie Seward Barry, *Visual Intelligence: Perception, Image, and Manipulation in Visual Communication* (Albany, NY: State University of New York Press, 1997).

13. Kurt Lang and Gladys Engel Lang, "The Unique Perspective of Television and Its Effects: A Pilot Study," *American Sociological Review* 18 (1953): 3–12.

14. Lynda Lee Kaid, Craig Corgan, and Phil Clampitt, "Perceptions of a Political Campaign Event: Media vs. Personal Viewing," *Journal of Broadcasting* 30 (1976): 303–12.

15. The Pew Research Center for the People and the Press. (August 17, 2008). Audience Segments in a Changing News Environment: Key News Audiences Now Blend Online and Traditional Sources. 2008 Pew Research Center Biennial News Consumption Survey.

16. Michael X. Delli Carpini and Scott Keeter, *What Americans Know about Politics and Why It Matters* (New Haven, CT: Yale University Press, 1996).

17. John P. Robinson and Mark R. Levy, *The Main Source: Learning from Television News* (Beverly Hills: Sage, 1986).

18. Bernard C. Cohen, *The Press and Foreign Policy* (Princeton, NJ: Princeton University Press, 1963), 13.

19. Maxwell E. McCombs and Donald L. Shaw, "The Agenda-Setting Function of Mass Media," *Public Opinion Quarterly* 36(2) (Summer 1972): 176–87.

20. David Weaver, Maxwell McCombs, and Donald L. Shaw, "Agenda-Setting Research: Issues, Attributes, and Influences," in *Handbook of Political Communication Research*, ed. Lynda Lee Kaid (Mahwah, NJ: Lawrence Erlbaum, 2004), 257–82.

21. Everett M. Rogers, James W. Dearing, and Dorine Bregman, "The Anatomy of Agenda-Setting Research," *Journal of Communication* 43(2) (1993): 68–84.

22. James W. Dearing and Everett M. Rogers, *Agenda-Setting* (Thousand Oaks, Calif.: Sage, 1996).

23. Weaver, McCombs, and Shaw, "Agenda-Setting."

24. See Weaver, McCombs, and Shaw, "Agenda-Setting."

25. Maxwell E. McCombs, Sheldon Gilbert, and Chaim Eyal, "The State of The Union Address and the Press Agenda: A Replication." Paper presented at the annual meeting of the International Communication Association, Boston, MA (1982).

26. Leon V. Sigal, *Reporters and Officials: The Organization and Politics of Newsmaking* (Lexington, MA: D. C. Heath, 1973).

27. Sigal, *Reporters and Officials.*

28. For a review, see Weaver, McCombs, and Shaw, "Agenda-Setting."

29. Shanto Iyengar and Donald R. Kinder, *News That Matters: Television and American Opinion* (Chicago: University of Chicago Press, 1988), 63.

30. Iyengar and Kinder, *News That Matters,* 114–15.

31. Robert M. Entman, "Framing: Toward Clarification of a Fractured Paradigm," *Journal of Communication* 43(4) (1993): 51–58, 52.

32. Thomas E. Nelson, Rosalee A. Clawson, and Zoe M. Oxley, "Media Framing of a Civil Liberties Conflict and Its Effect on Tolerance," *American Political Science Review* 91(3) (September 1997): 567.

33. Johnson-Cartee, *News Narratives.*

34. Bennett, *News,* 125.

35. Frank I. Luntz, *Candidates, Consultants, and Campaigns: The Style and Substance of American Electioneering* (New York: B. Blackwell, 1988); Bruce I. Newman and Richard M. Perloff, "Political Marketing: Theory, Research, and Application," in *Handbook of Political Communication Research,* ed. Lynda Lee Kaid (Mahwah, NJ: Lawrence Erlbaum, 2004): 17–44.

36. Robert Schmuhl, *Statecraft and Stagecraft: American Political Life in the Age of Personality* (Notre Dame, IN: University of Notre Dame Press, 1990), 4.

37. *Frontline: The Persuaders,* DVD, directed by Barak Goodman and Rachel Dretzin (Alexandria, VA, PBS Video, 2004). Available online at http://www.pbs.org/wgbh/pages/frontline/shows/persuaders.

38. Ronald Berkman and Laura W. Kitch, *Politics in the Media Age* (New York: McGraw Hill, 1986), 121.

39. James David Barber, *The Pulse of Politics: Electing Presidents in the Media Age* (New York: W. W. Norton, 1980), 8.

40. Timothy E. Cook, *Governing with the News: the News Media as a Political Institution* (Chicago: University of Chicago Press, 1998).

41. Thomas E. Patterson and Robert D. McClure, *The Unseeing Eye: The Myth of Television Power in National Politics* (New York: Putnam, 1976).

42. Roderick P. Hart, *Seducing America: How Television Charms the Modern Voter* (Thousand Oaks, CA: Sage, 1999).

43. Lynda Lee Kaid, "Political Advertising," in *Handbook of Political Communication Research,* ed. Lynda Lee Kaid (Mahwah, NJ: Lawrence Erlbaum, 2004), 155–202.

44. Michael Griffin, "Camera as Witness, Image as Sign: The Study of Visual Communication in Communication Research," in *Communication Yearbook 24,* ed. William Gudykunst (Thousand Oaks, CA: Sage, 2000), 433–63.

45. Doris A. Graber, "Political Languages," in *Handbook of Political Communication,* ed. Dan Nimmo and Keith Sanders (Beverly Hills, CA: Sage, 1981), 212.

46. See 1968 figure from Daniel C. Hallin, "Sound Bite News: Television Coverage of Elections, 1968–1988," *Journal of Communication* 42(2) (2004): 5–24, figure from Eric P. Bucy and Maria E. Grabe, "Taking Television Seriously: A Sound and Image Bite Analysis of Presidential Campaign Coverage, 1992–2004," *Journal of Communication* 57 (2007): 652–75.

47. See also Lowry and Shidler's discussion of "video bites" and Masters, Frey, and Bente's "visual quotes:" Dennis T. Lowry and Jon A. Shidler, "The Sound Bites, the Biters, and the Bitten: A Two-Campaign Test of the Anti-Incumbent Bias Hypothesis in Network TV News," *Journalism & Mass Communication Quarterly* 75 (1998): 719–29; Roger D. Masters, Siegfried Frey, and Gary Bente, "Dominance and Attention: Images of Leaders in German, French, and American TV News," *Polity* 25 (1991): 373–94.

48. Bucy and Grabe, "Taking Television Seriously."

49. See Kathleen Hall Jamieson, *Packaging the Presidency* (New York: Oxford University Press, 1996).

50. Theodore H. White, *The Making of the President, 1960* (New York: Atheneum Publishers, 1996).

51. Time, "We Get the Picture," *Time* (October 4, 1993).

52. Anne Marie Barry, "Perception Theory," in *Handbook of Visual Communication*, ed. Ken Smith, Susan Moriarty, Gretchen Barbatsis, and Keith Kenney (Mahwah, NJ: Erlbaum, 2005), 45–62.

53. Antonio Damasio, *The Feeling of What Happens: Body and Emotion in the Making of Consciousness* (New York: Harcourt, 1999).

54. Anne Marie Barry, *Visual Intelligence: Perception, Image, and Manipulation in Visual Communication* (Albany: State University of New York Press, 1997); Paul Messaris *Visual Persuasion: The Role of Images in Advertising* (Thousand Oaks, CA: Sage, 1997).

55. J. Anthony Blair, "The Possibility and Actuality of Visual Arguments," *Argumentation and Advocacy* 33 (1996): 23–39, 23.

56. Shawn W. Rosenberg, Lisa Bohan, Patrick McCafferty, and Kevin Harris, "The Image and the Vote: The Effect of Candidate Presentation on Voter Preference," *American Journal of Political Science* 30(2) (1986): 108–27, 123.

57. Doris A. Graber, *Processing Politics: Learning from Television in the Internet Age* (Chicago: The University of Chicago Press, 2001); Allan Paivio, *Imagery and Verbal Processes* (Hillsdale, NJ: Lawrence Erlbaum, 1979).

58. John E. Newhagen and Byron Reeves, "This Evening's Bad News: Effects of Compelling Negative Television News Images on Memory," *Journal of Communication* 42(2) (1992): 25–41.

59. John E. Newhagen, "TV News Images that Induce Anger, Fear, and Disgust: Effects on Approach-Avoidance and Memory," *Journal of Broadcasting and Electronic Media* 42 (1998): 265–76.

60. Colin Berry and Hans-Bernd Brosius, "Multiple Effects of Visual Format on TV News Learning," *Applied Cognitive Psychology* 5 (1991): 519–28; Hans-Bernd Brosius, "Format Effects on Comprehension of Television News," *Journalism Quarterly* 68(3) (1991): 396–401; Hans-Bernd Brosius, "The Effects of Emotional Pictures in Television News," *Communication Research* 20(1) (1993): 105–24; Hans-Bernd Brosius, Wolfgang

Donsback, and Monika Birk, "How Do Text-Picture Relations Affect the Informational Effectiveness of Television Newscasts," *Journal of Broadcasting and Electronic Media* 40 (1996): 180–95; Mickie Edwardson, Donald Grooms, and Steve Proudlove, "Television News Information Gain from Interesting Video vs. Talking Heads," *Journal of Broadcasting* 25(1) (1981): 12–24; Olle Findah, "The Effect of Visual Illustrations upon Perception and Retention of News Programmes" *Communications* 7 (1981): 151–67.

61. Doris A. Graber, "Seeing Is Remembering: How Visuals Contribute to Learning from Television News," *Journal of Communication* 40(3) (1990): 134–55; Doris A. Graber, "Say It with Pictures," *The Annals of the American Academy* 546 (1996): 85–96.

62. Philip Kipper, "Television Camera Movement as a Source of Perceptual Information," *Journal of Broadcasting and Electronic Media* 30(3) (1986): 295–307.

63. Daniel M. Shea and Michael John Burton, *Campaign Craft: The Strategies, Tactics, and Art of Political Campaign Management* (Westport, CT: Praeger Publishers, 2001).

64. Dan G. Drew and Thomas Grimes, "Audio-Visual Redundancy and TV News Recall," *Communication Research* 14 (1987): 452–61; Thomas Grimes, "Mild Auditory-Visual Dissonance in Television News May Exceed Viewer Attentional Capacity," *Human Communication Research* 18 (1991): 268–98; Annie Lang, "Defining Audio/Video Redundancy from a Limited Capacity Information Processing Perspective," *Communication Research* 22 (1995): 86–115.

65. Robert M. Krauss, William Apple, Nancy Morency, Charlotte Wenzel, and Ward Winton, "Verbal, Vocal, and Visible Factors in Judgments of Another's Affect," *Journal of Personality and Social Psychology* 40(2) (1981): 312–20.

66. Patricia Noller, "Video Primacy—A Further Look," *Journal of Nonverbal Behavior* 9(1) (1985): 28–47; Michael I. Posner, Mary J. Nissen, and Raymond M. Klein, "Visual Dominance: An Information-Processing Account of Its Origins and Significance," *Psychological Review* 83 (1976): 157–71.

67. Cited in Gunter Schweiger and Michaela Adami, (1999). "The Nonverbal Image of Politicians and Political Parties," in *Handbook of Political Marketing*, ed. Bruce I. Newman (Thousand Oaks, CA: Sage, 1999), 347–64.

68. John S. Nelson and G. R. Boyton, *Video Rhetorics: Televised Advertising in American Politics.* (Chicago: University of Illinois Press, 1997), 90, 94.

69. Samuel L. Popkin, *The Reasoning Voter: Communication and Persuasion in Presidential Campaigns* (2nd ed.) (Chicago: University of Chicago Press, 1994), 9.

70. Victor C. Ottati and Robert S. Wyer, "Affect and Political Judgment," in *Explorations in Political Psychology*, ed. Shanto Iyenger and William J. McGuire (Durham, NC: Duke University Press, 1993), 296–316.

71. Graber, *Processing Politics.*

72. Richard E. Petty and John T. Cacioppo, *Communication and Persuasion: Central and Peripheral Routes to Attitude Change* (New York: Springer-Verlag, 1986); Alice H. Eagly and Shelly Chaiken, *The Psychology of Attitudes* (Fort Worth, TX: Harcourt Brace Jovanovich College Publishers, 1993).

CHAPTER 2

Media Events

A media event is an event that has been staged to produce press coverage and influence public opinion. In a media event, newsmakers attempt to control every element of the event through careful scripting and staging, rigid rules, and cautious press management. Media events are constructed to obtain news coverage, communicate a favorable message clearly and quickly, and influence viewers. They are simple in message and format, and use colorful characters and visual to produce iconic images. The intended audience for a media event is the audience at home watching the event on television and reading about it online and in newspapers; the direct audience attending the event in person is seen more as a prop than as a group of voters to influence. Candidates attempt to make news and to be picked up by network and cable news programs by arranging speeches, rallies, and press conferences in friendly and personal settings to give the press the visuals and storylines they need for the night's political coverage. Newsmakers use media events because they limit risk and allow candidates to control important elements in a message. As noted journalism critic Philip Seib describes: "When a candidate appears at rallies, delivers public speeches, and performs other such campaign duties, he remains in almost total control. These heavily planned events allow him to say what he wants to say, look how he wants to look, and generally present the image of his choice to the voter."[1]

Media events now play a fundamental purpose in setting the media agenda and influencing the media frames of candidates and issues. The media event is one of the primary tools used in political campaigns, and increasingly, in government. This focus of this chapter is on the media event itself through a discussion of structural changes in the political process that have increased the importance of events, the common types of media events, and the media event tactics communication consultants use to improve the likelihood of success of their events.

Structural Changes Favoring Media Events

Public appearances and photo opportunities have been a common part of political campaigns for centuries. In his autobiography, Benjamin Franklin confesses to employing self-dramatization in his campaign, and in the 1840 presidential election between Martin Van Buren and William Henry Harrison, Harrison (an affluent descendent of Virginia aristocracy with a distinguished military record) ran a substance-less campaign based on songs, symbols, slogans, and myth.[2] While image-making has long been a part of the political process, changes in our media and electoral system have increased the importance of staged media events. This shift from retail politics and public address toward media events occurred for several reasons. The most important factor leading to the rise of the media event is the integration of television into political affairs. As Berkman and Kitch describe: "If any factor has changed the modern campaign trail, it is the presence of the television camera. In the modern campaign, the candidate does not have to hustle from place to place, shaking hands, kissing babies, repeating the same speech over and over again. Media events can be staged."[3]

The modern media event emerged and evolved in concurrence with the popularity of television. In the 1968 campaign, Richard Nixon was one of the first politicians to understand the role of television in politics and carefully constructed his image through media events.[4] In the later phases of his campaign, Nixon staged several elaborate town-hall style media events designed to show he was an engaged leader connected to the problems of the day. Also in the 1968 presidential campaign, Senator Eugene McCarthy staged several media events including walking along the beach, a visit to the elderly, and a plant gate appearance.[5] Today, no event is held without first considering how the event will appear on television and staging the event around those constraints.

Second, the relationship between journalists and the newsmakers they cover has also evolved over time into a complicated and uncomfortable partnership. Larry Speakes, acting White House Press Secretary for Reagan, made this point clear through a telling tongue-in-cheek sign that he kept on his desk that read, "You don't tell us how to stage the news and we don't tell you how to cover it."[6] While the relationship can be adversarial, this distrust is often present in name only because what is good for the candidate is typically what is good for the reporter. Both campaigns and the news media want an interesting story, compelling pictures, and large number of viewers. News media gatekeepers look for stories that are simple, dramatic, personal, predictable, and easy-to-cover under deadline constraints.

Third, as political parties have become less important and the news media has assumed the role of symbolic kingmaker, PR specialists have become more important, and the media events they promote, are now a central element in campaigns at all levels. Communications specialists and public relations consultants have increased in both sophistication and influence. News management is now both an art and a science practiced by a powerful group of professional consultants who work with politicians of both parties. The permanent campaign phenomenon has further raised the importance of media events and marketing techniques have been imported from campaigns into the legislative and governing arenas.

Fourth, the news media are now faced with a 24-hour news cycle—there is a constant demand for news. The news hole—the number of pages or minutes of news required every publishing cycle—has increased with advent of 24/7 cable news and is seemingly endless with the ubiquity of online news sources and blogs. Campaigns are able to capitalize on this need by providing media events that are designed to be fashioned into stories with a minimum amount of effort. Anderson and Van Winkle (1976) describe this process:

> There is another way in which television's hunger for filmable incidents can affect the course of a campaign. For several years now the astute campaign managers have realized that what a candidate does on the stump may be far less effective than what he does on television, especially what he can manage to do on television news programs. There he is relieved of the expense of commercials, freed of the taint of image making, and he appears in a context of credibility. His campaign incidents thus have the aura of news. These managers have also discovered that local televisions need to "fill up" their one-hour evening news shows and can be fairly easily seduced into covering almost any incident which makes good pictures. Hence the arrival of the pseudo event as standard campaign procedure, a happening devised to attract television coverage in good time to be processed and edited for the evening news programs. In effect, television is asking the campaign "please fill this space." Campaign managers adept at that will benefit.[7]

Campaign managers understand the language of news and provide media events that fit that language.

Fifth, as news outlets are increasingly purchased by media conglomerates, the logic of corporate profit has overtaken traditional news values. Economic pressures have always been a part of journalism, but changes in the last 20 years has placed new strains on the press. The news business is primarily concerned with the bottom line—how to achieve the highest ratings with the lowest amount of cost to benefit corporate owners and shareholders. To increase ratings, news content shifts to info-tainment, brief sound and image bites, and self-promotion, and news is homogenized to appeal to the audiences sought after by advertisers without offense. At the same time, to lower costs, media staffs are cut, television, print, and radio are conglomerated, and small outlets are forced out of the marketplace. Political coverage, especially on the more partisan cable networks, has shifted after from a straight news, "just the facts" format to one dominated by partisan talking heads like Bill O'Reilly and Keith Olbermann. To keep the shows visually interesting, these programs display montages of images of the candidates at media events—called b-roll—instead of airing long shots of the commentators speaking to the camera, which further privileges media events. These changes have made it easier for newsmakers to use media events to their advantage.

Sixth, reporters rarely deviate from the news narrative that has been established. Looking at reports of the same event from different news agencies, the coverage is striking predictable, similar, and homogenous. It is as if the stories were all written and shot by the same reporter—reports usually use a familiar frame and will feature similar leads and sound bites, the same images, and the same issues. As advanceman Patrick Halley argues, "The reporters working the event tend to keep one another honest since no one wants to have to explain to his editor why his account was different."[8]

Finally, several subtle changes in the newsgathering process have made contributed to the prominence of media events. For example, it is commonplace for reporters and producers to stage shots, set up events that are photogenic, and otherwise fake video.[9] This staging acclimates the staging of events and makes the staging of media events a normal part of newsgathering. New technologies have also allowed media events to dictate the news. The use of live trucks and satellite news has forced correspondents to quickly edit their coverage without accompanying analysis. Accusations of media bias have also removed some power from the news media to interpret and explain stage-managed events as they attempt to remain objective. The more objective the report, the greater advantage received by the organization staging an event because reporters become stenographers for the campaign.

Media events have become a primary communication tactic for presidents and presidential candidates, and other newsmakers including governors, senators, and house members. Media events are now so ingrained into our political culture that they are a daily concern for both newsmakers and the press. Major leaders almost never appear without the choreography of their advance staff. Candidates and elected officials do not only campaign by media event; they often govern by media event. It is not limited to campaign communication, when going public in support of a policy, presidents and other leaders do so by staging appearances in battleground states in an attempt to move public opinion in their favor. Where events are perhaps the most important is during presidential elections. The sheer number of media events in a presidential campaign is staggering. From August 24 to November 6, 2000, Bush made a total of 133 campaign appearances, Gore made 100, while vice-presidential candidates Dick Cheney and Joe Lieberman made 112 and 94 appearances, respectively.[10] In total, the presidential and vice presidential candidates made 439 campaign appearances in the final months of the 2000 campaign. The numbers were similar in 2004 as Bush made 123 appearances compared to 102 appearances by Kerry from September 3 to November 1, 2004. In that year, Cheney made 114 appearances while Democratic vice presidential nominee John Edwards held 123 appearances. Combined, the presidential and vice presidential candidates made 462 appearances in the fall of 2004.

The only extensive study of media events was conducted by Daniel Boorstin in *The Image: A Guide to Understanding Pseudo-Events in America* in 1961 (the book was originally titled *The Image or What Happened to the American Dream*).[11] In *The Image*, Boorstin argues that Americans are becoming detached from their reality by a commercial and political system that favors the imagined over the real—that our demand for news and image-based culture has left us without a compass. Boorstin created the term "pseudo-event" to describe any staged event that creates a synthetic novelty for news and public consumption, such as an interview, a press conference, a photo opportunity, or televised debate. For Boorstin, a pseudo-event possesses four characteristics: it is planned or incited, its primary purpose is to be covered by the news media, it is ambiguously related to the reality of the situation, and it is a self-fulfilling prophecy.

Since Boorstin's initial study, the term pseudo-event has been narrowed to mean any fully controlled presentation designed for media consumption—what today's political consultants and news reporters would term a "media event." Media events and pseudo-events are two different phenomena and it is important not to conflate the concepts. Using the terms interchangeably deviates from and misuses Boorstin's original concept and limits his argument. Further, this pejoration of all media events into pseudo-events gives a negative connotation to all media events which is unwarranted and incorrect. Some extreme media events are pseudo-events, but not all media events are pseudo-events. We should also be careful not to comingle the definition of media event used by political practitioners and the concept of a media event popularized by media scholars Daniel Dayan and Elihu Katz.[12] Dayan and Katz define a media event as any event that attracts prominent coverage by news organizations from the assassination and funeral of John F. Kennedy to the royal wedding of Charles and Diana to the Olympics. While that is an important concept, it is distinct from the term media event as used in political contexts and the two usages of the term are separate and discrete.

Types of Media Events

Media events are standardized and typically follow one of the following stock formats: the speech, the press conference, the town hall, the issue event, the niche event, the "spontaneous" event, the cabinet and congressional contact event, the arts, culture, or social event, the state visit, the foreign trip, and the special event.

THE SPEECH

When we think of media events, speeches are usually the first to come to mind. Staged speeches provide maximum control for newsmakers because everything from the backdrops to the crowds to the remarks themselves can be managed on a second-by-second basis. Where candidates once stood on stumps, porches, or rickety platforms, newsmakers today rely on million dollar sound stages and lighting, audio, and cinematographic techniques borrowed from Hollywood. As detailed in later chapters, developing and executing a major speech today requires a highly trained staff and often weeks of planning.

THE PRESS CONFERENCE

Perhaps the most direct way to reach the news media; press conferences are used to access the media agenda. In a press conference, a newsmaker invites reporters to hear them speak and will usually take questions from the reporters. Press conferences allow candidates to focus attention on a specific issue and address a large number of journalists at once. Typically, a newsmaker will begin with a brief opening statement summarizing their view on the issue of the day and anticipating press questions, followed by a period of questions from the journalists in attendance.

THE TOWN HALL

A variation of the press conference is the town hall, in which the newsmaker takes questions from the assembled audience. The speaker usually dispenses with the podium and instead roams the audience with a handheld microphone. These events are used to communicate a message of honesty and candor by showing the candidate seemingly answering any question, even these questions are often screened in advance or given to audience members. Because the candidate has stepped off the stage, these town halls depict the candidate as down to earth and "of the people." John McCain built his 2000 and 2008 campaigns for the Republican nomination around these town halls. In open public forums and aboard his campaign bus, the *Straight Talk Express*, McCain gave the press and primary voters nearly unlimited access to him, and upset front runners by demonstrating his frankness and comfort level with the issues. Importantly, when McCain was criticized for ineffective events in June of 2008, he hired staging specialists from the Bush White House and switched his event strategy from free flowing town halls to heavily scripted speeches and issue events.[13] At one point in August of 2008, McCain, the candidate known for open access to the press and informal events, went four weeks without a press conference and three weeks without a public town hall meeting.[14]

THE ISSUE EVENT

As the name suggests, issue events are held to attract attention to and advocate for a specific political issue or political cause. These appearances usually take the name of the issue at the center of the event—newsmakers hold "social security events," "environmental events," or "jobs events." For example, memos from the Reagan White House show the administration organizing multiple events to make the environment a major issue. In those memos, Mike Deaver and the advance office proposed several possible events, such as presenting the World Wildlife Fund Prizes to the 1983 Winners, attending a "Save the Condors" fundraiser, dropping by the "New EPA," or visiting the Forest Rangers Training School, a National Park, or a toxic waste disposal site.[15] The potential strengths for each media event were discussed in the memo, for instance, the toxic waste disposal event "would show the Presidents concern about toxic waste and demonstrate that it can be safely disposed of" while a visit to a coal fired plant using a clean scrubbing system would serve a dual purpose because it would appeal to blue-collar workers in addition to its environmental focus.

THE NICHE EVENT

Events are also scripted to target and reach specific audiences and demographic groups on calculated issues. White House advance and scheduling offices maintain lists of possible events for various constituencies such as blue-collar workers, women, Catholics, Hispanics, and senior citizens that they can employ as political situations dictate. Advance staffers also refer to these niche events with one word labels based on the targeted audience: "women event," "Catholic event," "Hispanic event," "elderly event," and so on. For example, to interest various minority groups during the 1972 campaign, Nixon planners were advised to be aware of opportunities to hold regional ethnic events: "watch for days like Pulaski Day which means something to a certain group and program them in."[16] Similarly, to appeal to the working class, Ronald Reagan's staff recommend attending a baseball game as "attendance at an all American event such as this would surely improve his image with the blue collar people at home drinking beer in front of the television set," eating at a McDonalds because "if we are trying to appeal to the blue collar constituency, we should eat the food of the blue collar constituency," and stopping by a local fire station to "provide good photos with these working class 'heroes.'"[17] To influence other groups, the memo continues, Reagan could hold different events: for women, Reagan could visit a child care center; for Hispanics, the president could drop by the Little Havana section of Miami; for Catholics, he could deliver a television broadcast on Christmas.

THE "SPONTANEOUS EVENT"

The ironically named "spontaneous events" are scripted to look unplanned and spur-of-the-moment. Mixed in with press conferences and formal speeches in a campaign trip are more unstructured events to place the newsmaker in more relaxed and casual settings and to generate action-oriented pictures for the traveling press. As a 1971 memo to all Nixon advance men reminds, "always have a planned 'spontaneous' stop along the motorcade route."[18] Often, these events are not listed on the publicly distributed schedule or on the schedule provided to the press. Advance staffers are always on the lookout for interesting and visually compelling settings to position the candidate. A strategy directive between Nixon's top advisors reveals this strategy: "The spontaneous and perhaps unusual facets of the trip should be actively pursued. Such 'unplanned' activities such as visits to the Ohio State campus, going out shopping for ties, and stopping by a factory along a motorcade route, all show the personal side of the President and create more of the public impressions necessary to reach out to all people. Scheduling in planning for a trip should provide the flexibility, where possible to pursue these spontaneous activities."[19]

THE CABINET AND CONGRESSIONAL CONTACT EVENT

These events, in which the president is shown meeting with his cabinet or congressional leaders, are designed to show the president at work and to provide pictures for news stories that may not be inherently visual. An example of this type of event would be a staged meeting with the president and his or her foreign policy advisors to presumptively discuss an ongoing crisis in international affairs. Similarly, when the president is advocating for his positions in the House or Senate, he or she may stage event with leaders in those legislative bodies to demonstrate his commitment to working with Congress. When traveling, presidents and candidates may also hold contact events with heads of state or local and state leaders such as mayors and governors.

THE ARTS, CULTURE, OR SOCIAL EVENT

One of the most frequently staged events in the White House is the social event. Social events are held daily to accomplish various purposes. Social events can be used to promote a social, cultural, artistic, or athletic cause, such as meeting with children who have completed a reading program or presenting national arts and humanities medals. They can also be used to communicate the human side of the presidency by placing the president with children or other groups, such as the annual White House Easter Egg Roll, or in social settings such as the annual holiday celebrations for Christmas. As a memo about social events from the Nixon administration describes: "White House social events should radiate excitement and a festive air. They should suggest a sense of well-being in the world and subtly say that the President is in command and that there is a reason for entertainment and enjoyment."[20] Nixon himself was engaged in the planning and outcomes of these ceremonial events, as this memo from chief of staff H. R. Haldeman to scheduler Dwight Chapin confirms: "The President was pleased with the public response to his appearance at the Azalea Festival and feels that we should try to find a way every week or so to set up some kind of activity for him that will show people being friendly and responding enthusiastically."[21] Nixon, like other presidents, used ceremonial and social events for political purposes. These events are not solely for entertainment, they also serve political purposes.

THE STATE VISIT

A state visit is a formal social event in which the president invites and welcomes the head of state of another country to the White House. State visits allow presidents to symbolically play the role of president and demonstrate diplomatic allegiances. At a minimum these events include contact events with the foreign leader, but can be expanded to incorporate joint press conferences, ceremonial events such as welcoming ceremonies, state dinners, and trips to national landmarks or cultural events.

THE FOREIGN TRIP

International summits and other diplomatic proceedings are another common type of media event which is carefully staged. These events depict the president or candidate performing on an international stage and impart stateliness and gravity to the newsmaker. When the president represents the nation abroad, he assumes the presidential role and can capitalize on the symbolic trappings of the position. International summits typically include group press conferences, meetings open to the press, a "class photo" event in which the leaders stand on risers to be photographed, and so-called grip and grin events of the leaders happily shaking hands. Often, these events have multiple audiences such as citizens and leaders of the host country, heads of state in adversary countries, and Americans at home. Because of this, international summits are perhaps the most carefully scripted of all media events. For instance, a memo from Carter White House Communications Director Jerry Rafshoon to the president before the Vienna Summit in which the Strategic Arms Limitation Talks II (SALT II) agreement was ratified emphasizes the tone and communication tactics Carter should employ, including nonverbal messages such as clothing, photographs, and demeanor. Regarding demeanor, Rafshoon writes, "Don't smile. Don't act as if you and (Soviet leader Leonid) Brezhnev are friends. (Above all, don't say that you are.) At the meetings—particularly when you're being photographed—try to look at Brezhnev the way you look at me when I walk into your office. The image should be toughness, not gentleness."[22] Here again we see candidates and their staffs considering, planning, and managing every symbolic message.

An especially potent foreign event is a fact-finding trip to a war zone to learn about the situation on the ground and visit with the troops. These events allow the president to take on the commander in chief role and surround themselves with patriotic symbols, as further described later in the book. Just as Americans rally around the flag and troops at a time of war, this type of photo-op encourages voters to rally behind the president. Newsmakers frequently employ this type of event to boost their approval ratings and exhibit leadership characteristics. As described in the introduction, George W. Bush frequently returned to this type of event to strengthen his image during the lengthy war on terrorism.

THE SPECIAL EVENT

There is a final category of event encompassing large special events such as the quadrennial presidential nominating conventions and multistate campaign trips. Much has been written describing the evolution of political conventions from nominee selection and party ratification meetings to mass media spectaculars. Conventions today are carefully stage managed to energize the party faithful and persuade undecided voters via the ensuing blitz of media coverage. Research has shown the effectiveness of conventions in influencing public opinion and most candidates receive a "convention bump" in surveys. Similarly, in throwbacks to the celebrated Whistle-Stop campaigns of earlier campaigns, candidates now frequently stage marathon bus, train, airplane, and boat tours. In 1988 George H. W. Bush and Dan Quayle made headlines by arriving in New Orleans by riverboat for the 1988 Republican Convention. Bill Clinton and Al Gore did one better in 1992 and 1996 by scripting multistate, made-for-pictures bus tours after the Democratic Convention to capitalize on a post convention bounce. In an analogous event 2000, Democratic candidates Al Gore and Joe Lieberman channeled Mark Twain and cruised the Mississippi River by paddle boat after the convention—holding events in the riverside towns and cities in the battleground states of Wisconsin, Illinois, Iowa, and Missouri.

Media Event Tactics

Overtime, a common set of media event tactics has been developed to improve the likelihood that each event will not only receive coverage, but also that the resulting coverage will more likely be positive. The next section considers these strategies, including: making news, fulfilling the media need for dramatic pictures, including the press in the planning of events, managing logistics for the press, using media-friendly timing, and traveling. The detailed strategy and tactics of planning specific events, such as crowd building and backdrops are included in the follow chapter on advance.

MAKING NEWS

The first media event tactic is to "make news" by providing convenient and newsworthy events for the press that follow the norms and conventions of what is news. Each day, the news media has a "news hole" to fill and the rise of the 24-hour cable news networks has only increased this need for content. Media events can be used to prepackage this content in a manner that is easily digestible to the press. Specifically, to maximize positive coverage, each event must offer something new—a new issue, a new comment, a new visual, or a new attack. Events should have a "news peg" or hook that demonstrates to editors and journalists that the event is newsworthy. Media event planners must also consider the daily routines of the press corps and be attuned to routinely staging events to satisfy the media's daily need for news. We see this emphasis in a memo from the LBJ administration, wherein staff assistant Charles Maguire reminded Jack Valenti and others planning LBJ's schedule that their events must be mediagenic: "travel, even Presidential travel, can be pedestrian. We should contrive to make every visit an event—and dramatic in setting, original in style, newsworthy in execution and intent."[23]

Perhaps the most successful of the White House to use this technique was the Reagan administration. Reagan's communication group attempted to "make news" and manage the news on a daily basis. They would limit their focus to a single "message of the day" and schedule events to drive home that message. You can regularly see this focus in memos sent between communication aides. For example, in a spring 1982 memo titled "A New Offensive" from David Gergen to Jim Baker, Ed Meese, Mike Deaver, and Bill Clark, Gergen argued for increased efforts in managing the news. Gergen argues that several steps are needed: "1. Promulgation of new rules on photo ops, press availabilities, etc. . . . 2. News planning—. . . There is no excuse for us as an administration not to have at least one fresh domestic story and one foreign one from the White House each week—and hopefully more."[24] This memo shows the administration attempting to make news with at least one new story each week. It should be noted that while Reagan's team focused on making news, arguably the news media were willing participants in Reagan's news management operation. While individual reporters occasionally decried Reagan's techniques, the majority bent over backwards and covered the events as scripted by the White House.[25] Deaver and his colleagues were happy to fill this need and enticed the press with good pictures, drama, and personality in their events. Deaver and the advance staff thought of themselves as producers of the nightly news and it was their goal to make an image so good that the press would have to use it.[26]

FULFILLING THE MEDIA NEED FOR DRAMATIC PICTURES

Each event is also constructed to be mediagenic and offer the press and viewers at home interesting pictures accompanied by dramatic storylines. The media uses standard news values to select which stories are covered and which are not; events that are visual, dramatic, significant, personal, clear, and timely are more likely to be covered than those that are not, so events are staged to capitalize on those news values.[27] To ensure pictures from an event make the evening news or the next day's paper, each event is constructed to be colorful, visually interesting, properly framed, and correctly lit for still photography and videotaping. As the Nixon advance manual makes clear:

> Every Presidential appearance is at least partially symbolic in nature. Both the live and television audiences will have their interpretations of what is happening affected by a multitude of factors such as the size, nature, and temperament of the crowd, the response of the audience to the President's remarks, and even by such apparently insignificant factors as the manner in which the hand signs are painted, the appearance of the hall and the quality of the decorations. The Ad-

vanceman must insure that all of these factors work to the advantage
of the President and he must always remember that the televised effect
take top priority. Though thousands may be in the live audience they
are a small group compared to the millions of television viewers.[28]

In the world of modern television news, for there to be a story, there must be a
visual. As noted by Schmuhl, "Television is a medium highly dependent on engaging pictures. There is a visual imperative."[29] So if a candidate seeks coverage,
they must satisfy that visual imperative and stage an event to provide that visual.
Similarly, if a story is unfavorable, visuals should be controlled to ensure that a
negative story will not have an accompanying negative visual. As longtime correspondent Jim Lederman notes, "Television news is enslaved to images. If an
idea cannot be recorded in the form of an image, it will rarely, if ever, be given
extensive time on a nightly network newscast."[30] While a campaign cannot directly control how a story is covered or a reporter's voiceover during a news package, campaigns can control the images that are available and make certain those
images are favorable. Matthew Bennett, former trip director for Al Gore, makes
this point, arguing that "we can't control the decisions made by the writer or editor about what will be covered. . . . If the media wanted to run a 'horse race
story' and Al Gore wanted to talk about policy, the advance team can at least
convey the intended message visually."[31] Hillary Clinton consultant Patrick Halley similarly argued that, "A good rule of thumb is that the media are going to
highlight the most interesting picture you provide for them,"[32] so if a politician
wants an event covered, the advance staff must supply appealing images.

Reagan press secretary Larry Speakes explains that this focus on providing
compelling pictures to the media was a major element of their communication
strategy:

> Underlying our whole theory of disseminating information in the
> White House was our knowledge that the American people get their
> news and form judgments based largely on what they see on televi-
> sion. We knew that television had to have pictures to present its story.
> We learned very quickly that when we were presenting a story or try-
> ing to get our viewpoint across, we had to think like a television pro-
> ducer. And that is a minute and thirty seconds of pictures to tell the
> story, and a good solid sound bite with some news. When Reagan was
> pushing education, the visual was of him sitting at a little desk and
> talking to a group of students, or with the football team and some
> cheerleaders, or in a science lab. Then we would have an educators'
> forum where the President would make a newsworthy statement. We
> knew very quickly that the rule was no pictures, no television piece,
> no matter how important our news was. If we saw nothing on the
> President's schedule that would make the evening news that night, we

would say, "No coverage." And if the press didn't like it, the press didn't like it. There was no need to have cameras in there and reporters trying to ask questions that would embarrass the President unless we could get our story on TV.[33]

Using visuals to drive a story was common before Reagan, and it has become universal and ubiquitous in political communication today.

As described in the introduction, you can see the Bush administration's focus on the visual throughout his presidency. For example, when Bush spoke about jobs for low working Americans, VIPs seated behind the president were instructed to remove their neckties so Bush would appear as a man "of the people" on television;[34] when Bush spoke at Mount Rushmore, his staff moved the camera platform so his face would be visually superimposed on the mountain when viewed on television; and when speaking in New York City, Bush's staff rented barges full of stadium lights to majestically illuminate the Statue of Liberty as a backdrop.[35] Of course, Bush is not the only politician strategically controlling their backdrops and visual images. In one notable media event in August 2003, Democratic presidential candidate Howard Dean spoke in front of a campaign created graffiti-painted background in Manhattan's Bryant Park in an attempt to reach out to young voters.[36]

INCLUDING THE PRESS IN THE PLANNING OF EVENTS

Both the White House and the traveling press corps have similar goals; they want to produce dramatic stories featuring compelling pictures of the president that will attract viewers. These mutual purposes often result in the White House advance office and press corps working together to construct events. From memos in the presidential libraries, it is clear that often the press assists the White House in staging events—specifically, helping set up camera angles and planning the visual elements of events. Obviously, the logic employed by newsmakers is that the more the press is involved in the planning of events, the more likely the candidate will receive favorable coverage from those media outlets. Documents from the George H. W. Bush library demonstrate the closeness between the White House and the media. Representative from each of the major media outlets participated in pre-advance trips and assisted the Bush Communications Office in planning and designing foreign trips, Diana Walker, White House photographer for *Time* magazine, contributed to pre-advance work for the 1990 NATO Summit in London and helped design the events to maximize the visual appeal of the events and ensure that the locations made for good photographs. In a memo to be distributed to photographers, Walker describes each event in detail such as the optimal lens to be used and the physical layout of each event, including copies of the photographs she shot during the advance.[37] A similar memo from the 1984 Republican Convention planning group to McManus and Deaver regarding the design and color of the convention podium reports that photographers from *Newsweek* and *U.S. News & World Report* inspected a model of the convention hall and "were favorably impressed with the design, and the consensus was that the earth tones are very attractive and will appear 'warm and comfortable' in still shots."[38] While it is difficult to judge the effectiveness of this tactic because these efforts are largely behind the scenes and reporters are not likely to admit to being influenced by this technique, it is worth noting the tactic was used and acknowledged by the presidential communication teams.

MANAGING LOGISTICS FOR THE PRESS

The communication and advance operations not only attempt to influence the public debate by creating the symbolic elements within events; they also manage the logistics for the press to make it easy to cover the event as staged and nearly impossible to challenge the pro-candidate frame of the event. Schedules are developed to allow ample time for writing, editing, and submitting stories, but not enough time for the press to leave the controlled events and obtain competing perspectives and still meet their deadlines. This coordination includes technical details such as lighting, sound, platforms, telephones, and Internet access, as well as planning and managing basic tasks such as the schedule, transportation, lodging on overnight trips, writing and editing time and space, and food.

Event planners see a link between keeping the news media happy and literally well fed, and their ability to feed the press favorable news. This focus is clear from the LBJ advance manual instructions on supervising the mostly male press corps on the late 1960s: "If your stop is near a meal time, provide an area nearby the platform but out of view of the cameras with sandwiches and light refreshments for the press and necessary staff. If the motorcade route is lengthy, provide pretty girls and light snacks on the buses especially for press."[39] Similarly, although less directly, the Reagan advance manual suggests developing an amiable environment for the media: "The thrust of the Press Advanceman's responsibilities is to develop and implement both the creative aspects and the functional logistical press arrangements for Presidential events. The goal is to create an atmosphere and setting that will provide favorable media coverage by both the national traveling press and the local media."[40] The Reagan advance office believed that arranging and controlling event sites was the most critical and variable aspect of events: "this is where judgments as to camera angles (relationship of crowd to president), writing press area, communications proximity, routes for press, staff, and VIP movements become critical. It is at a speech site, where the news is actually being made—that the tone of the trip is set."[41] In other words, if the logistics for the press are handled smoothly and the event is unproblematic, the resulting coverage will advantage the president.

Advance manuals direct campaign staffers to be helpful and practical in their interactions with the press with a focus on making it easy to cover the event as scripted and difficult to challenge the campaign framing of an event. For example, the Nixon advance manual instructs the advance staff to be straightforward with the press and make their job effortless: "Conflicts will arise only if the press advanceman has made unrealistic arrangements, changed the ground rules to favor certain individuals, or has lost sight that even though the local media are important, the national press and the pool are much, much more important. The press will be fair to the press advanceman if they feel that the press advanceman is fair to them. Many of the media will do their job in the easiest manner possible, and they expect the advanceman to make their job easy."[42] The Carter advance manual is not as optimistic in describing how to deal with the press, warning the advance staff to be prepared for reporters' aggressiveness. The manual reads: "The Advance person's major concern, after finalizing the schedule and building crowds, is to help publicize the visit by helping the press. This task will often wear your patience thin. Their needs for mechanical facilities are many and exacting. Their interest in covering the Candidate's visit often clashes with your interest in conserving his time and the Secret Service's interest in reducing hazards to his safety. Finally, their eagerness for eye-catching headlines may clash with the campaign's desire for full and balanced coverage. Just as reporters compete fiercely with each other, expect them to do so with you."[43] In addition to dealing with logistics for journalists, advance men and women must also manage reporters' personalities and egos.

USING MEDIA-FRIENDLY TIMING

Events are also timed to maximize their influence on the public agenda. Each day reporters must gather information, interview sources, write their piece, and edit the final product—all on a strict deadline. Depending on the event and the desired coverage, different timing is used by the event planners. If an event is large enough to receive live media coverage, the event is timed to air during the morning news shows or for a primetime audience. If an event is smaller, the event may be held midday so reporters have sufficient time to assemble their story but limited time to interpret and filter the message away from the desired message of the event. Political events are scheduled around the media time lines, especially those of television. Fred Dutton, Deputy National Chairman for Lyndon Johnson's 1964 campaign, makes this point in 1964 in a memo to Bill Moyers: "In terms of present day communications, which is the real problem at hand, we are in the age of mass media, especially television—not the whistlestops and political rituals dear to most of our hearts but really part of a period that went out with Truman as far as the overwhelming majority of people are concerned."[44] This focus on scheduling political events around television can also been seen in strategy documents from the Nixon administration, like this one from H. R. Haldeman: "In developing the weekly game plan for the President, it is extremely important that major emphasis be given to TV coverage as well as general news releases. In other words, the game plan should look specifically at stories that are slanted to TV and that will be given major television play."[45] As Clinton political consultant James Carville has observed, "In this business you haven't said anything until you've said it on television."[46]

Conventions, one of the largest and most elaborately staged of all events, have completely changed over the past 50 years to conform to the schedule of television. Memos between Nixon staffers made clear that they understood how television was impacting the political process. One memo on the 1972 Republican Convention reminds planners of the centrality of television in the convention: "The convention must be built around the use of television rather than having television serve the convention."[47] This focus on the media over other concerns can also be seen in a strategy memo regarding the 1984 Republican National Convention from the Reagan Library. After presenting three possible event scenarios in a memo for Deaver to review and select, advanceman William Henkel makes an argument for one option over the others because of the television coverage that would result: "This scenario maximizes prime time network coverage. It assumes that an event scheduled earlier in the day will provide the networks with a story for their evening news. I am confident the networks would cover the President's arrival in Dallas as well as the hotel rally, both of which coincide with prime time network programming and routine convention business."[48] As this memo demonstrates, a principal concern when staging these events is how the timing of the event will be the most convenient story for the television networks.

A second way to maximize media timing is to piggyback events on issues that are already in the news. Holding events on historical anniversaries or national days of celebration is especially common, especially for the president. Reagan's visit to Normandy, France, for the 40th anniversary of D-Day is one such example of a president riding issues that were already important to Americans. Included in the speechwriting files in the Reagan library are extensive press clippings on the upcoming D-Day anniversary which where presumably used to plan their events and set them in their appropriate contexts. Americans would have likely rallied around the World War II veterans with or without Reagan, but when the president appeared at Pointe du Hoc and Omaha Beach, the country also rallied around the commander in chief. Reagan's communication staff also took advantage of popular support on other issues in the public agenda such as the Olympic Games, National Christmas Tree lighting ceremonies, and the rededication of the Statue of Liberty.

TRAVELING

Another media event tactic used by the president is to leave Washington, D.C., and hold events around the country to bypass the national press corps and reach out to local and regional media affiliates. These outlets are thought to be less critical and more likely to cover an event as scripted without negative commentary than the more cynical White House press who covers the president every day. Traveling also gives the president the opportunity to "act presidential" in mediagenic settings around the country and surround themselves with the symbolic trappings of the office, such as Air Force One, motorcades, and the Secret Service. In the same way, foreign travel allows the president to build their image at home by representing the country as a head of state, while correspondingly immobilizing critics who are leery to attack a president on foreign soil. The Ford advance manual describes this tactic to his event planning staff: "More often than not, a primary reason for a Presidential trip is to show the nation's leader in an environment other than his oval office in Washington, D.C. The only way to achieve this is to make certain that the press is always in a position to capture the flavor and setting that the advanceman has gone to such great length to insure . . . and then making certain that the reporters can file the story."[49]

Advance manuals describe several specific techniques that could be used to generate free press coverage in the local media, such as releasing announcements and supplemental press releases, holding press briefings, publicizing the First Lady's participation, and creating human interest or "side-bar" stories through press releases. One of the most common methods of making these feature stories was by promoting the arrival of Air Force One, as highlighted in the Reagan advance manual: "The public loves details about how a Presidential visit works, and loves to see the Secret Service agents, the cars, and all the rest almost as much as they want to see the President. Therefore, the advanceman should spark an interest among the populace in turning out to see the 'historic event.'"[50]

Traveling is a major concentration for every modern president and you can see this in documents in their archives. The Johnson Library in particular has several interesting memos discussing "going public." For example, a memo from Bill Moyers to President Johnson advocates for this strategy: "When the President chooses a locale outside of Washington to talk about world affairs or domestic issues, the regional newspapers give it extra play. The President has favored them by making his pronouncements in their area, and whatever he says is bound to be accepted much more favorably. Regional pride affects these papers deeply."[51] The memo continues with Moyers arguing that traveling can also influence public opinion on an issue, which in turn helps to motivate congressional votes. "This is another good way to move the Congress. A President draws his strength from the people. Each time you go out to the people you return with a renewal of the mandate. If the people are convinced, their legislators are much easier to convince." President Johnson's handwritten notes on the document approve the policy, indicating its importance as a communication strategy. Later in his presidency, the administration returns to this approach as a response to shifting public opinion on Vietnam. In a memo to President Johnson in March of 1966, special assistant Jack Valenti argues that LBJ should take several "planned, carefully planned" trips outside of Washington to "show the President in contact with the people, so that regional news stories help bring the President closer to ordinary citizen" and "to tell the story of Vietnam in such a way as to enlarge public support for the Administration position—and stop the polarization of public opinion."[52]

Local and region media outlets can also be approached without traveling, a tactic used widely by the Reagan administration. For example, on May 23, 1983 alone, President Reagan met with handicapped Girl Scouts from San Diego, a chess team from Indianapolis, and the mayor of Rocky Mount, North Carolina. Pool cameras distributed the footage from these events and it resulted in positive television and print coverage in San Diego, Indianapolis, and Raleigh.[53] These human interest or soft stories with local news value put the president into American homes—if not nationally, at least in targeted areas—each day on the local six o'clock news. In another instance, Reagan held a special concert at Disneyworld for high school bands that were unable to play at his inauguration due to inclement weather. Reagan capitalized on the poor weather during his inauguration to stage a second media event—not only could the local press cover their community bands' involvement in his inauguration; they could also cover the make-up concert in Florida.

Reviewing local television and newspaper coverage shows the success of this traveling strategy. Through the 1980s and 1990s, local media would typically cover a president visit to their town in a nonstop fashion—they would carry the president's arrival, speech, and motorcade live—and would often write stories in the days leading up to and after the event. Reagan advisor Deaver explained the logic of this tactic: "We were playing to local markets. We plotted it out to overlay [what were] key political states for us with major media markets: Atlanta, Dallas, Los Angeles, Chicago, St. Louis, Boston. You'd have two days of stories before the President arrived, about the security and logistics and all that, then they'd cover the actual day of the President's visit."[54] While traveling is still a widely used strategy, local and regional press have largely adopted the style of the national press and are now less likely to give fawning coverage of the president. Decreases in small newsroom staffs and budgets have also limited the amount of coverage a president receives when traveling.

Conclusion

This chapter introduced and examined the basic elements of the media event; one of the most ubiquitous yet understudied elements of modern political communication. Because of fundamental changes in how politicians reach out to voters and how the news media covers political affairs, the media event has increased in importance and candidates campaign largely through media events and increasingly rely on media events to communicate when in office. A set of stock media event types has emerged and event planners draw on a familiar collection of tactics to influence reporters and voters. The subsequent chapters elaborate on this focus and take a closer look at the advance staff and the communication specialists that plan and manage these events, how these events function, and the impact of media events on the public sphere.

Notes

1. Philip M. Seib, *Who's in Charge?: How the Media Shape News and Politicians Win Votes* (Dallas: Taylor, 1987), 33–34.

2. Robert Schmuhl, *Statecraft and Stagecraft: American Political Life in the Age of Personality* (Notre Dame, IN: University of Notre Dame Press, 1990).

3. Ronald Berkman and Laura W. Kitch, *Politics in the Media Age* (New York: McGraw Hill, 1986), 120.

4. Joe McGinniss, *The Selling of the President, 1968* (New York: Trident Press, 1969).

5. Robert Agranoff, *The Management of Election Campaigns* (Boston: Holbrook, 1976).

6. Larry Speakes and Robert Pack, *Speaking Out: The Reagan Presidency from Inside the White House* (New York: Scribner, 1988).

7. Vernon F. Anderson and Roger Van Winkle, *In the Arena: The Care and Feeding of American Politics* (New York: Harper & Row, 1976), 369–70.

8. Patrick S. Halley, *On the Road with Hillary: A Behind-the-Scenes Look at the Journey from Arkansas to the U.S. Senate* (New York: Viking, 2002), 23.

9. Bonnie Anderson, *News Flash: Journalism, Infotainment, and the Bottom-Line Business of Broadcast News* (1st ed.) (San Francisco: Jossey-Bass, 2004).

10. Daron R. Shaw, *The Race to 270: The Electoral College and the Campaign Strategies of 2000 and 2004* (Chicago: The University of Chicago Press, 2006).

11. Daniel J. Boorstin, *The Image: A Guide to Pseudo-Events in America* (New York: Harper & Row, 1964).

12. Daniel Dayan and Elihu Katz, *Media Events: The Live Broadcasting of History* (Cambridge, MA: Harvard University Press, 1992).

13. Sasha Issenberg, "On Campaign Trail, Stage Presence Takes Center Stage," *Boston Globe* (August 10, 2008).

14. Mosheh Oinounou, "McCain Embraces the Staged Rally," Fox Embed, FoxNews.com (September 10, 2008).

15. Memo, Environmental Commission Plan, Reagan Library.

16. Memo, General Assumptions-Travel, folder: Schedule Planning 1971, box 25, WHSF: Chapin, Nixon Presidential Materials.

17. Memo, Constituency Oriented Events, Reagan Library.

18. Memo, Walker to All Advancement, 10 September 1971, folder: The Presidential Advance Manual 1971, box 387, WHSF: Haldeman, Nixon Presidential Materials.

19. Memo, Chapin to Haldeman, 22 January 1971, folder: Scheduling Planning 1971, box 25, WHSF: Chapin, Nixon Presidential Materials.

20. Memo, Chapin to Haldeman, 22 January 1971, folder: Scheduling Planning 1971, box 25, WHSF: Chapin, Nixon Presidential Materials.

21. Memo, Haldeman to Chapin, 28 April 1969, folder: Memo from HRH 1969, box 18, WHSF: Chapin, Nixon Presidential Materials.

22. Memo, Rafshoon to Carter, 8 June 1979, folder: Memoranda from Jerry Rafshoon—June, July, and August, 1979, box 28, Office Files of Greg Schneider, Carter Library.

23. Memo, Maguire to Valenti, 1 February 1966, folder: Trips 6-24-65–3-15-66, box 1, WHCF: Trips 11-22-63, LBJ Library.

24. Memo, A New Offensive, Reagan Library.

25. See also Mark Hertsgaard, *On Bended Knee: The Press and the Reagan Presidency* (Rev. ed.) (New York: Schocken Books, 1989); Mark Hertsgaard, "Ronald Reagan: Beloved by the Media," *The Nation* (June 28, 2004); John Anthony Maltese, *Spin Control: The White House Office of Communications and the Management of Presidential News* (2nd ed.) (Chapel Hill: University of North Carolina Press, 1994); Schmuhl, *Stagecraft*.

26. Bill Moyers, *The Public Mind: Illusions of News* (Alexandria, VA: PBS Video, 1989).

27. See Kathleen Hall Jamieson and Karlyn Kohrs Campbell, *The Interplay of Influence: News, Advertising, Politics, and the Internet* (Belmont, CA: Wadsworth, 2005).

28. Advance Manual, folder: Advance Manual (1), box 1, Rosenberger-Blaser Papers, Ford Library.

29. Schmuhl, *Stagecraft*, 87.

30. Jim Lederman, *Battle Lines: The American Media and the Intifada* (New York: Henry Holt, 1992), 132.

31. Cited in Daniel M. Shea and Michael John Burton, *Campaign Craft: The Strategies, Tactics, and Art of Political Campaign Management* (Rev. and expanded ed.) (Westport, CT: Praeger, 2001), 178.

32. Halley, *On the Road*, 19.

33. Speakes and Pack, *Speaking Out*.

34. Jim Shella, "Some Audience Members Told Not to Wear Ties for Bush Speech," *WISH-TV 8* (May 15, 2003).

35. Elizabeth Bumiller, "Keepers of Bush Image Lift Stagecraft to New Heights," *New York Times* (May 16, 2003).

36. Joseph Dolman, "Dean Isn't New York's Kind of Connoisseur," *Newsday* (September 3, 2003).

37. Turfbuilders Report, Diana Walker, folder: NATO Summit London England 7/4-7/90, Office Files of John Herrick, Bush Library.

38. Memo, Convention Update, Reagan Library.

39. Checklist for Advance Operations, folder: Advance Men, box 1, Office Files of James R. Jones, LBJ Library.

40. Advance Operations Manual, 1981, folder "Advance Office Operations Manual," box 19325, William Henkel Files, Ronald Reagan Library, 203.

41. Advance Operations Manual, 1985, folder "Advance Operations Manual (Master)," box OA 11359, Office of Presidential Advance Records, Ronald Reagan Library, 204.

42. Advance Manual Revision, folder: Advance Manual Revision re "The Press" Ch. VIII (2), box 1, Rosenberger-Blaser Papers, Ford Library.

43. Carter/Mondale Advance Manual, folder: Advance Manual, box 1, Jody Powell Papers, Carter Library.

44. Memo, Dutton to Moyers, 26 September 1964, folder: Campaign, box 53, Office Files of Bill Moyers, LBJ Library.

45. Memo, Haldeman to Butterfield, 20 March 1969, folder: Memo from HRH 1969, box 18, WHSF: Chapin, Nixon Presidential Materials.

46. Quoted in Lloyd Grove, "How Experts Fueled a Race with Vitriol," *Washington Post* (January 18, 1989), A14.

47. Memo, Gavin to Shakespeare, 10 February 1971, folder: Republican National Convention-Television, box 25, WHSF: Chapin, Nixon Presidential Materials.

48. Memo, 1984 Republican National Convention Survey, Reagan Library.

49. Advance Manual, folder: Advance Manual (1), box 1, Rosenberger-Blaser Papers, Ford Library.

50. Advance Operations Manual, Reagan Library, 194.

51. Memo, Moyers to Johnson, 25 January 1966, folder: Trips 6-24-65–3-15-66, box 1, WHCF: Trips 11-22-63, LBJ Library.

52. Memo, Valenti to Johnson, 5 March 1966, folder: Trips 6-24-65–3-15-66, box 1, WHCF: Trips 11-22-63, LBJ Library.

53. Memo, Coverage by locals on 5-23-83, Reagan Library.

54. Cited in Hertsgaard, *On Bended Knee*, 49–50.

CHAPTER 3

Advance

Advance is perhaps the least known and most misunderstood position in a White House administration or political campaign. The modern concept of advance in politics was popularized by Jerry Bruno, who earned a reputation as a maverick when working as John F. Kennedy's advanceman. In his book, Bruno describes in great detail how he went from driving a forklift at an American Motors plant to planning events for the president. Bruno immortalized the role of advanceman through story after story of screaming crowds, strong-armed local politicians, foreign travel, and ticker tape parades. Bruno summarizes his role in a campaign:

> It's my job in a campaign to decide where a rally should be held, how a candidate can best use his time getting from an airport to that rally, who should sit next to him and chat with him quietly in his hotel room before or after a political speech, and who should be kept as far away as possible. It's also my job to make sure that a public appearance goes well—a big crowd, an enthusiastic crowd, with bands and signs, a motorcade that is mobbed by enthusiastic supporters, a day in which a candidate sees and is seen by as many people as possible—and at the same time have it all properly recorded by the press and their cameras.[1]

Later advance workers used Bruno as a model when staging events.[2] In summary, it is the role of the advance person to heavily script and stage events that appear unplanned to benefit their candidate. As Agranoff explains, "All of the advanced events are designed to create the impression that the appearance of the candidate triggered an outpouring of enthusiasm and support for the candidate. One cynic has thus labeled the work of advanceman as planned spontaneity."[3]

Unlike other campaign strategies, advance is not taught in schools, instead, advance strategies and tactics are passed down through word-of-mouth and dog-eared advance manuals, one-day seminars at the start of a campaign, and apprentice-like relationships. The nature of the work tends to attract creative, decisive, independent types willing to work long hours and live out of suitcases, constantly on the road. As the advance manual used in the Nixon and Ford administrations explains:

> [The advanceman's] authority and responsibilities are awesome. He possesses a rare combination of characteristics and abilities: he is the decision maker graced with a tremendous amount of common sense and good judgment; he is diplomatic yet forceful; he has the ability to anticipate and think of things in their total context and not get bogged down in petty details, he is resourceful and has a unique ability to organize people, things and his own time; he has the answers; in short, he can get the job done in a manner becoming a personal representative of the President. Yet the Presidential Advanceman must accomplish these things in an anonymous fashion—he must have a passion for anonymity—giving gladly all the credit for a successful visit to the local people.[4]

Hillary Clinton advanceman Patrick Halley similarly observes that, "The job attracts mavericks, hyper, creative, seat-of-the-pants types, who roar into town on all cylinders and expect everyone to get out of their way."[5] And in his memoir, Charles Stuart, an advanceman for Nixon in the 1968 campaign who also planned several foreign trips, compares advancemen to Charles Dickens's artful dodger, "Most importantly, you have to be the kind of person whose motto was, 'first we get into the stadium, then we change for better seats.'"[6] Because of this, advancemen and -women form a unique fraternity. Somewhat like magicians, advance workers work in the background and are not meant to reveal their secrets and rarely publicize their role. For this reason, the role and effect of advance on political communication is relatively unexplored.

This chapter considers the advanceman's role in political communication by first examining the necessary skills required to work advance and the advanceman's job description. This chapter then expands on these basic skills by describing the steps in advancing an event and the communication tactics advance people can use to make the event more mediagenic and improve the probability that the news media will favorably cover the event and voters will come away with a positive impression of the candidate or elected official. The chapter concludes with a discussion of black advance—a type of counteradvance designed to work against advancemen.

The Advanceman or Advancewoman

An advanceman or advancewoman is a campaign professional who designs, creates, and manages the creative and functional elements of a media event.

The goal for the advance staffer is to create an atmosphere and event setting that will generate favorable media coverage by both the national traveling press and the local media. The advance staff has three primary goals, as the Jimmy Carter advance manual spells out: "The advance must strive to be sure that: the candidate communicated the best and most appropriate message to the greatest number of potential voters, that the media were enabled to capture and project the candidate's ideas to the largest possible audience, (and) that the local hosts, politicians and voters are left with a favorable impression of the candidate and his views."[7] The most important goal is to place the candidate in a mediagenic setting which will communicate the desired message to likely voters. Second, the advance person must manage the media and encourage and cast the candidate in favorable terms. Last, the advance person must be a diplomat with the local politicians and voters so that the event energizes voters and the local political machine to support the candidate. In each task, ensuring that the smallest detail works to the advantage of the candidate is paramount, according to George H. W. Bush's advance manual: "Relentless attention to detail is what advance work is about." Completing these three different tasks requires combining various skills and job roles—the advance person must be at once a scheduler, a negotiator, a volunteer coordinator, an event planner and crowd builder, a visual speechwriter, and a television producer.

The Reagan advance manual provides a good job description of multi-faceted nature of advance work:

> *Advancing is an art!* It is the exhaustive, detailed planning that makes each Presidential trip and event appear to be an *effortless* success. An incredible diversity of activities is involved: organizing the efforts of local citizens or sponsoring groups anxious to host the President; publicizing the President's impending visit; decided where and how the President will go; working with the White House support team on a myriad of details from press coverage to motorcades; coordinating the audio/visual requirements with the White House Communications Agency; assisting and guiding local efforts to provide the proper atmosphere; providing suggestions and guidance on the use of "color" to add a tenor of dignity, gaiety, and/or spontaneity to a visit; arranging for the right people to be in all the right places at the right time; meeting with governors, mayors and business and labor leaders and working with them in such a manner that they feel comfortable and at ease around the President. While following what the schedule requires; and above all, anticipating potential problems and having solutions available![8]

And all of these jobs must ideally take place in the background without the media or the voting public recognizing the advance person's work. Clearly, this is a complex staff position with multiple responsibilities; let us next consider each element in the advanceman's job description in turn.

THE ADVANCEMAN AS SCHEDULER

It is important to recognize that scheduling has a *communication* function; the selection and timing of events and appearances reinforces the candidate's message and contributes to the candidate's political image. Working in concert with other areas of the campaign and the scheduling office or coordinator, the first task of an advanceman is to scout potential events for the candidate's schedule and determine which events have the most symbolic and political potential. Ideas for events come in from all areas of a political organization—from constituent letters and e-mails to lobbyist requests—and the advance office evaluates the strengths and weaknesses of each event. As part of this role as scheduler, the advanceman or Advance Office acts as the information center when the event draws closer, including formulating event concepts with the scheduling and appointments director, determining the physical and logistical requirements for the press, and proposing a minute-by-minute schedule of each event for the chief of staff. In the White House, the advance person must also coordinate each event with the Chief of Staff, the United States Secret Service, the White House Press Office, Political Affairs, Congressional Affairs, Intergovernmental Affairs, Communications, and Speechwriting offices.

THE ADVANCEMAN AS NEGOTIATOR

In a national campaign, the goals of the advance office, which must represent the national position of the campaign, often conflicts with priorities of local politicians or field staffers. While the local host would likely schedule the candidate for 24 hours a day, the advance person must protect the candidate's time and prioritize events that best serve the message of the campaign. For example, a local political leader may want to hold a jobs event at a factory owned by a prominent donor but the national message scheduled for that day is healthcare. In a situation such as this, the advance person must step in and gracefully represent the national campaign, plan the healthcare event, and gain the support of local volunteers and staffers. The advance person is the diplomatic middleman between the local hosts, politicians, and vendors and the candidate's staff. The Carter advance manual summarizes this role: "His challenge, both as a technician and as diplomat, is to mesh the legitimate needs of many persons—local hosts, candidate, his staff, local and travelling press, Secret Service, and Advance Desk—into a visit which will be successful both logistically and politically."[9] To complicate matters, advancemen often try to have the local or state party absorb as much of the cost of the event as possible to save the campaign money, which inevitably causes friction with the local hosts. One way advance staff alleviates this friction is by making sure the local hosts always receive the credit when events go well.

THE ADVANCEMAN AS VOLUNTEER COORDINATOR

Of course, a major media event could not be created in a matter of hours by one person, so a major part of the job is finding, energizing, and managing hundreds of volunteers. If the advance person is the general, the soldiers are a cadre of enthusiastic amateurs. After selecting a site, the advance staffer will start creating an entire hierarchy of volunteers. Party loyalists and previous volunteers are given chairmanships and given lists of tasks to complete, depending on the job. For a major presidential campaign or event, volunteers will be needed to chair groups focusing on publicity, media logistics, entertainment and programming, parking, crowd building, facilities, the platform party and VIPs, the motorcade and cars, hotel and airport arrangements, and signs and banners. These committee chairs are often not dedicated to the event or capable of handling the scope of the tasks, so it is up to the advance person to check and double check the committee chairs. Because of compressed timelines, chairs are never given a second chance if they make a mistake and these chairs will be dismissed for simply showing up to a meeting without a pen and paper. The lead advance must have full confidence in each chairperson. Since volunteers are frequently government employees covered by the Hatch Act, volunteers may not be able to participate in partisan or fundraising activities.

THE ADVANCEMAN AS EVENT PLANNER AND CROWD BUILDER

Once major decisions have been made and the volunteer operation has been established, the advance person's attention shifts to the logistics of an event. The advance team must not only consider what the candidate will say, they also attempt to control every other symbolic element of the event, such as the setting, the crowd, and the pictures and video that would run in the news media following the event. The best advancemen and -women understand that you can, in the words of Reagan advanceman James Hooley, "integrate the message, the agenda, the president's policy goals, into the event. You can take the atmosphere, the venue, the locale, the people that are in the photograph . . . so that it all reinforced the message."[10] Everything must be planned to the smallest detail and carried out with precision: Should the signs be hand-painted or professionally printed?; What color should the backdrop be?; Do we have sandwiches for the press?; What song should play when the candidate is working the rope line? It is the responsibility of each advanceman to address these types of questions and develop a minute-by-minute schedule of each event, considering the candidate or politician's message, audience, and setting to construct an event that positively develops both the candidate's agenda and image. Advance manuals are largely instructions about how to handle these details. The Nixon advance manual has a forty page checklist of items for the advance staff to complete when planning a presidential trip. For example, when picking a rally site, an advanceman should consider over twenty items, such as the number of seats for the crowd, the buildings physical appearance, parking availability, fire regulations, the convenience of motorcade access, the sound system, the lighting system, and the enthusiasm of the arena management.[11] Much of an advance representative's time is spent on seemingly mundane but important logistical details like arranging hotel rooms, transporting luggage, setting up transportation and motorcades, organizing office space, and testing every microphone, door, and chair. Yet if any of these details are overlooked, it may result in a failed event and negative coverage of the candidate.

THE ADVANCEMAN AS VISUAL SPEECHWRITER

Just as a speechwriter composes the words a candidate will say, the advance person "writes" the nonverbal and visual symbolic elements of a speech. This includes staging elaborate backdrops to reinforce the message, surrounding the candidate with crowds to indicate popularity and momentum, playing appropriate music, and managing and encouraging the news media to favorably cover the event. The advance person must think in "image bites" and understand what their audience—the news media—is looking for in a story. Specifically, they must consider the news values the media is looking for in an event and what types of visual images grab the attention of photographers and editors and favorably frames the candidate and their issues. The goal here is to create a scene that is so photogenic and powerful that the press cannot help but shoot the event and include the video or photographs in their stories covering the event. Advance staffers want a single photo to tell the story of what the candidate was doing, why he was there, who he was speaking to, and the purpose of the visit. George H. W. Bush's advance manual pushes their advancemen and women to focus on these images: "One photograph can, with attention to content and creativity, send a message that words can neither deny nor expand upon." This focus on the visual is evident in the Reagan advance manual:

> *Remember Details, Television Does.* Every Presidential appearance is partially symbolic. Both live and television audiences will have different interpretations of what occurs at an event, affected by a multitude of diverse factors. Included in, but not limited to, these factors are such things as the size, nature, and temperament of the audience; their responsiveness to the President's remarks; the layout and configuration of the facility; the quality of the decorations, etc. The advanceman should make every reasonable effort to ensure these factors work to the advantage of the President; with a particular eye towards capturing the "picture" of the event, pre-conceived during the "storyboard" analysis. The importance of staging, site choice, program content, etc. becomes critical.[12]

It is the responsibility of the advance person to visually *write* the event and create a mosaic of images that will hopefully influence voters watching on television. Just as a PR flack would write a press release, advance representatives create "visual press releases" via events.

THE ADVANCEMAN AS TELEVISION PRODUCER

Not only must an advance person stage the event for immediate audience at an event, they must also think about the secondary audience watching at home on television or seeing clips of the event on the Internet or evening news. Getting favorable images and stories on television is the primary consideration—everything else is a means to that end. As noted by the Nixon and Ford advance manual:

> Because of the overriding importance of the White House Press Corps, the careful thought and planning of their every move, every picture setup, every Presidential remark is one of the most critical aspects of a Presidential advance. It is a direct result of this advance planning that determines how the world sees the President. Without press coverage which accurately reflects what the Presidential Advance Team wants to illustrate, there is little reason for the President to make the trip.[13]

The Reagan advance manual is even more explicit on this point: "The final outcome of *any* event is determined, to a great extent, by the manner in which the press interprets it."[14] To this end, the advance person must think and act like a television producer to allow the press to easily and seamlessly cover an event.

This requires the advanceman to plan the event down to the second and prepare storyboards before an event to consider the camera angles that the press will require and that will benefit the candidate. The advanceman must understand the techniques, procedures, and conventions of the media, and follow those norms to garner positive media coverage, and consider, plan, and manage the physical and logistical requirements for the press. It is a series of unending questions: Are the colors in the backdrop camera friendly? Where will the satellite trucks park? How far is the cable run from the camera platform to the truck? What will the sun angle be at this time of day? And on and on.

There are several standard shots that are required by the press and that the advance person must consider when scripting the appearance. First, there is the wide establishing shot which takes in the entire event. Second and most importantly is the main camera platform which captures the headshot of the candidate speaking. Considerations for this shot include stage and camera platform location, the length of the camera throw and lens required for that distance, the camera platform angle, and the backdrop design and banner wording. Third, a "second position" or cut-away platform, so named because it is typically the second shot used in a television package, is necessary to give journalists a cut-away shot. This is usually done with a second platform placed at an angle approximately 45 degrees off the speaking position. For this second platform, the same issues must be considered: cut-away location, cut-away backdrop, and access between the two platforms. Last, the advance staff must plan for camera positions used by roaming photojournalists, often the "chute" area in front of the stage between the stage and the rope line. If the advance representative would like to highlight the size of the crowd or enormity of the event, an "over the shoulder" shot from behind the speaker may be staged to produces images of the enthusiastic crowd over the shoulder of the candidate. The advance staffer must ensure that all of the favorable symbolic elements that they stage are captured by the news media. "The key to covering a rally is to be aware of all the color events, such as balloon drops, confetti drops, signs, posters, etc. and be prepared to have the press pool in the proper position in the hall to catch (on film) the true atmosphere of the event," explains the Ford advance manual.[15] Other producer tasks include setting up camera platforms and the necessary electrical and audio and video equipment, properly lighting the stage and surrounding areas for television cameras, arranging for ample parking for the press and their satellite trucks, and equipping nearby "filing rooms" for the press with plenty of complimentary food and drinks. Of course, each media outlet will have their own producers and editors, but by preparing the event for the media it makes it easier for the press to cover the event and increases the likelihood of receiving positive media coverage. When the event begins, the advanceman shifts from producer to director. They typically stand at the off-stage entry point and coordinate the event using cell phones, radios, and runners.

Advance Process and Tactics

There are several basic steps in advance—an advanceman's work begins before the candidate's arrival at a city and ends after his departure. A message must be developed and a communication plan must be written, accompanied by an overall strategy and specific tactics designed to achieve that strategy in each event. Based on the plan, several media events are usually arranged, following a standard process. First, a survey report is developed through a "pre-advance" trip. In the survey report, the trip coordinator or lead advance person focuses on two areas. The first task is to assemble a brief profile of the area covering such information as demographic and economic data, political concerns, and local pride and concerns. This research allows the advance team to get the lay of the land, situate the event in its local context, and evaluate the strength of local and regional political groups. The second task is to appraise the geography and feasibility of possible settings for the event, including airports, routes, event sites, times, and possible hotels. This necessary step gives the trip coordinator several options about when, where, and how to stage an event. Optional events and sites are also designed and strengths and weaknesses for each potential event are evaluated. The key question in this report is "will [the] event accomplish [the] purpose(s) for the President's participation?"[16]

After a rough draft of the schedule has been outlined and the event locations selected, attention shifts to creating each individual event. For each event, an event plan is created to devise tactics to create the most favorable headline, picture, and story in media coverage of the event. The event is visualized considering elements such as staging, movements, the crowd, lighting, sound, parking, and public access. Reagan advanceman Hooley explains, "When you go out on an advance, your goal is to create the headline, picture, and the stories that are going to be running in the newspaper and on television."[17] Nearly every decision is guided by this analysis, from what the backdrop behind the candidate could read to what time of day the event could be held. Every element of the event is imbued with this message to make it difficult for the press, critics, or voters to interpret the event in any other way. Next, the advance representative assembles their advance team, typically using as many local representatives as possible. Local officials are consulted at nearly all stages of the advance process because they have local expertise and are helpful in building crowds. While local officials are consulted, the focus of the event is usually on the larger mediated audience and accommodating press requirements: "The timing and location of the event, the logistics, and the presentation can be designed according to the formats, the selection criteria, and the logistics of news reporting."[18]

Next, a site is selected that will be large enough to appear large in media coverage but small enough to easily fill and have an overflow crowd. Patrick Halley, Hillary Clinton's advanceman, summarizes the importance of site selection: "My biggest concern was building the crowd for the rally. It doesn't matter how many people actually show up; if the media report that the crowd size was 'disappointing' or show the deadly sight of empty seats, you have a failure. By the same token, if your crowd is described as 'large and enthusiastic,' it doesn't matter if it was made up of ten people dragged in off the street at the last minute. Success!"[19]

The next step is to script the event. This step includes developing a minute-by-minute schedule and drawing storyboards, like a film director, to conceive of the images the advance representative wants the press to photograph. Detailed diagrams of each event site are created from architectural drawings which use arrows and written instructions to show all movements, stage layouts, and seating charts at dinners. The advance rep uses gaffers tape to draw directional arrows on the floor for the candidate, staff, and media to follow and blocking markers on the stage floor to ensure the candidate is properly positioned for the lighting and cameras. After, the event is designed, promotion and crowd building begins. Last, it falls to the advance representative to manage the event—to make sure the band plays at the right time and the balloons are dropped when the speech crescendos. After the event, the advance staff is responsible for monitoring media coverage of the event and writing a summary report reviewing strengths, weaknesses, and lessons learned to be used when planning future events, and sending thank-you letters to everyone involved with the event. Once the work is done, it is advance tradition to hold a "wheels up" party after the conclusion of a successful trip or event. These parties serve two functions, first they allow the advancemen to review the event—what worked and what didn't—and make plans for future events. Second, the parties allow the advance team a chance to celebrate and relax after a stressful week of planning an event.

The advance person has several communication tactics in their toolbox that they can use to enhance the event and improve the likelihood that the press will favorably cover the event: having the candidate speak in a television friendly style, adding color, controlling candidate actions and gestures, surrounding the candidate with patriotic symbols, building and controlling crowds, inserting signs and banners, and controlling the setting and backdrop. The remainder of this chapter describes how advance staffs can use each of these tactics and how each functions in an event.

TELEVISION FRIENDLY REMARKS

In today's media event-based communication environment, what a candidate says is only part of a larger communication strategy. The words must match and support the message of the event, and the visual message communicated through the event must reinforce the candidate's spoken remarks. To accomplish this goal, modern presidents have coordinated and combined speechwriting and advance offices and considered both part of the overall media event approach. Care is taken to include several brief and dramatic lines in the president's remarks that reinforce the other elements of the event and could be used by the press as sound and image bites. Presidential libraries are full of memos reminding the advance and speechwriting offices to work in conjunction and encourage collaboration. The Reagan advance manual instructs: "Advancemen should always call the speechwriters to describe backdrops, local color and lore, ethnic make-up of the area, etc. This is very important."[20] One memo from early in the Nixon administration's first term illustrates this attempt at harmonization: "[The President] feels like there is a need for much closer coordination between the advance crew and the speech crew. For example, in South Dakota someone should have told Keogh or whoever wrote the speech something about the character of the crowd, the fact that they would be standing up; that it would be outside, etc., so that he knows what he is dealing with in the speech. . . . He feels it is hard to do a formal, read speech to a stand-up crowd, and he needs material that relates to the crowd, so the writer should get some color background on the type or kind of people, their interests, what they are expecting, etc."[21]

The master at using television friendly remarks to support a media event was Ronald Reagan. In an effort to get their desired viewpoint represented in the media, the Reagan administration ensured that the Great Communicator's remarks always supported the message of the day and followed the rules of a good sound bite. For example, in one noteworthy series of events in the 1984 presidential campaign, Reagan staged a whistle-stop tour following Harry Truman's historic route through Ohio on Truman's train, the *Ferdinand Magellan*, to tap into the Truman mystic and encourage Democratic voters to identify with Reagan. Reagan's stock speech that he delivered aboard Truman's train had several brief comparisons between himself and Truman and several attacks on Walter Mondale's policy as not fitting with the Democratic principles of the Truman era. From the back of the *Ferdinand Magellan*, the historic railcar used by Franklin Roosevelt, Dwight Eisenhower, and Harry Truman, Reagan proclaimed:

> Yes, I spent a great deal of my life as a Democrat. I respected Harry Truman's ability to stand for what he believes, his consistency of principles, and his determination to do the right thing. Mr. Truman could also make very plain the differences between himself and an opponent. And that's what I'm going to try to do today. . . . [Mondale's] tax increases to pay for his promises add up to the equivalent of $1,890 per household. If Harry Truman had to apply a motto to this radical taxing scheme, he'd have to say not "your buck stops here"—"your buck never stops."[22]

Analysis of the media coverage reveals that reporters frequently used these sound bites in their stories. For instance, the third paragraph of the *New York Times* story reads, "'Yes, I spent a great deal of my life as a Democrat,' Mr. Reagan told crowd after crowd along the 200-mile route. 'I respected Harry Truman's ability to stand for what he believes, his consistency of principles and his determination to do the right thing.'"[23] This sound bite or similar remarks were also featured in the *L.A. Times*, *Washington Post*, the *Dallas Morning News*, and the *Philadelphia Inquirer*, in addition to each of the three television networks. The president's remarks were part of the media event and were written to support the overall image-building theme for Reagan Democrats.

COLOR

While what a candidate says is critically important, the other nonverbal and visual symbols, referred to by advance staff simply as color, also play a central role in the overall message of an event. The press may only include a sentence from a candidate's remarks and viewers watching on television will likely not recall a candidate's sound bite; however, the setting, excitement, energy, crowd, and charisma cannot be ignored. The Carter advance manual refers to this color as "stardust": "It is the responsibility of the media advance to add 'stardust' to the ordinary event and thus lift it to a higher level of presentation. Obviously, not all events will lend themselves to special orchestration, however, sometimes the smallest little adjustments in the procedure will change the entire atmosphere."[24] Each president's advance manual is filled with suggestions of techniques to develop this color. The Nixon advance manual declares that "balloons excite crowds" and has six pages devoted to the intricacies of using balloons and discussing the comparative advantages of balloon rises, drops, releases, balloon mobiles, balloon trees, and barrage balloons. In the section on confetti, the same manual argues that more is always better: "How much Confetti?—The answer depends upon the specific area, but remember that the amount of confetti dropped is comparable to the bodies at a rally—there is always room for more!"[25]

The only modern president who strongly resisted this visual image making was Jimmy Carter. In response to President Carter's rejection of this visual image making, Carter's aides sent several memos to the president to attempt to persuade him to support the communication office's efforts to use color more frequently. A memo from White House Communications Director Jerry Rafshoon to President Carter argues that color is important because that is what interests the media: "The press has no interest in covering the content of these speeches—unless they break new ground. They do cover crowd reaction, mood, applause, delivery."[26] A similar memo from Jerry Rafshoon pushed the president to support the staff's image making: "You're going to have to start looking, talking and acting more like a leader if you're to be successful—even if it is artificial. Look at it this way: changing your position on issues to get votes is morally wrong; changing your style (like the part in your hair) in order to be effective is just smart, and in the long run, morally good."[27]

CANDIDATE GESTURES AND ACTIONS

A candidate's nonverbal behaviors, gestures, and actions can also be used to support an event's message. These gestures can range from the stereotypical baby-kissing to smiling and embracing supporters representative of important voting blocks. Candidate gestures and facial expressions are highly coached to appear active and open in their posture and supportive in their facial expressions. Candidates are trained to use the "point and wave" gesture before and after their speech. To appear active and engaged and demonstrate a connection to the crowd, candidates will find an audience member and point and wave in their direction, then shift to the other side of the audience and repeat the same gesture. You will also see candidates use this gesture when debarking from a campaign plane or bus; if there is no crowd, a staff member will leave the plane before the candidate and stand near the press, but off camera, so the candidate can point and wave and give the televised impression of a supportive crowd. This strategy reaches extremes after candidate debates, when all of the debaters can be seen simultaneously pointing and waving at the crowd in a strange ritual.

Presidents and presidential candidates must also worry about presenting a "presidential image" at all times—they must look and act the part—and avoid visual gaffes just as they would avoid verbal gaffes. To get a memorable image, advance people may advocate for arresting or eye-catching stunts, however, as the Reagan advance manual explains: "The advanceman must temper the mission of putting The President in a colorful and mediagenic setting while being cognizant of keeping The Presidential image intact."[28] Political history is littered with visual gaffes that have been exploited by the competition, such as when Michael Dukakis played soldier in a combat helmet and rode in a tank in a staged photo-op. It is the advance person's responsibility to prevent these embarrassing images. The Nixon advance manual humorously concludes with this reminder for advancemen:

> *The 37th President of the United States of America NEVER WEARS HATS* . . . no honorary hats . . . no protocol hats . . . no "great photo" hats . . . no "the law requires" hats . . . no "it's the custom" hats . . . no cute hats . . . no beanies . . . no stovepipes . . . no firehats . . . no captains hats . . . no caps . . . no Indian headdress . . . no feather hats . . . no hard hats . . . no soft hats . . . no ladies hats . . . no mens hats . . . no fur hats . . . no paper hats . . . no grass hats . . . no thorn hats . . . no "Nixon's The One" hats . . . no nothing. *HATS ARE TOXIC— AND CAN KILL YOU.*[29]

Obviously, a well-trained advance person knows to never put anything on a candidate's head.

The candidate can also be placed in action settings to show their personality and provide different images and backdrops for the press. The idea is that images of a candidate doing something are more powerful and memorable than a candidate speaking on the same topic, and more likely to receive media coverage. So instead of simply discussing the importance of technology and education, Bill Clinton and Al Gore attended a media event in which they helped wire a school for Internet access. This is a not a new strategy. Fred Dutton, Deputy National Chairman for Lyndon Johnson's 1964 campaign advocates for this strategy in a strategy memo:

> I consequently urge that the inevitable flood of speeches be intermingled as much as possible with action or doing situations. That should also help reinforce the emphasis on his ongoing Presidential role rather than candidate position.[30]

In the 2008 Democratic primaries, Barack Obama used various actions and gestures at three different stages of his candidacy as changes in the campaign necessitated different messages.[31] At the beginning of 2008, the Obama campaign relied on the question-and-answer town hall format to introduce the candidate and his issues in Iowa and New Hampshire. As momentum was building for his candidacy, he switched his strategy in Texas and Ohio and focused on large rallies in arenas that attracted fifteen to twenty thousand supporters. While these events helped establish his charismatic leadership style and demonstrated his popularity and momentum, they were less personal and allowed critics to paint Obama as out of touch with working-class, average voters. In the third phase of his campaign, he returned to an event strategy that mixed larger rallies with smaller town halls and action-oriented issue events. In Indiana, he invited the press to watch him roller-skate with his daughters, ate Subway sandwiches with an average-looking couple, had a conversation in a barn with a small group of farmers, visited seniors in a retirement home, and stopped by a VFW post to share a Budweiser with veterans. At one event at a family farm, Obama got off his campaign bus and presented his hosts with two apple pies before visiting with the family at a picnic table in their yard and sharing a basketball game in their driveway. These events are used to show the candidate's personality and dramatize the candidate's commitment to various groups of voters and their issues.

PATRIOTIC SYMBOLS

One of the most important image-building strategies of advance staff is to surround the president with core patriotic symbols such as the American flag. Patriotic symbols operate as a visual argument through association—when a candidate stands in front of the flag, viewers associate the candidate with their patriotic attitudes. Associating themselves with the flag allows candidates to transcend political differences and appeal to the nearly universal love for country. The basic tactic is to surround the candidate with as many patriotic symbols as possible in a mediagenic manner in an attempt to expose the audience to these symbols via the media. Flags are hung behind the candidate, passed out to the crowd, placed on buntings on ledges around the candidate, and used as the background on signs for the candidate. To present John McCain as a war hero and experienced senator in the 2008 campaign, McCain's advance staff frequently placed the candidate alone on the stage in front of a large flag, an image reminiscent of the iconic shot of George C. Scott in the film *Patton*.

Candidates appeal to patriotic symbols beyond the flag, such as Boy Scouts, brass bands playing Sousa songs, and high school cheerleaders. During the 2008 presidential campaign, Barack Obama combined all of theses symbols—flags, scouts, bands, cheerleaders—when he attended a small Fourth of July parade in working-class Butte, Montana.[32] Similarly, it has become commonplace for candidates campaigning in state primaries to appeal to the symbols of that state, so when in Iowa candidates attend the state fair and eat a funnel cake and when in Pennsylvania candidates partake in a Philly cheesesteak sandwich.

One memorable use of this tactic was by George H. W. Bush in the 1988 campaign against Democrat Michael Dukakis. Part of the Bush plan was to question Governor Dukakis's patriotism, in part because he had vetoed a bill that mandated the recitation of the Pledge of Allegiance in Massachusetts public schools. Bush made the flag a central element of every rally—surrounding himself with thousands of flags and ensuring that images from his rallies would prominently feature the flag. His communications team took this strategy to a new extreme when he held a media event at flag factories in Findlay, Ohio, and Roseland, New Jersey.

The Reagan PR apparatus also understood this strategy and did not hesitate to use any American symbol to perpetuate Reagan's desired "New Patriot" image. As the Reagan's Advance Operations manual instructed: "It's the flags, the signs and the confetti, the marching bands, the bunting, the Cubs Scouts and whatever other ingredients you can add, which will show a composite of what this country—and The President—are all about."[33] Reagan's advance staff apparently took this advice to heart because flags where a part of nearly every event. For example, Reagan's whistle-stop tour in the 1984 campaign was a montage of patriotic symbols—bands playing Sousa songs, flags hung from every post, and, of course, the train itself—which connected Reagan to his audience's shared history and experience.

In another memorable exchange, the Reagan administration actually engaged in a game of "capture the flag" with the Mondale campaign in 1984.[34] On the final day of their national convention in San Francisco, the Democrats staged a red, white, and blue, flag-waving spectacular. Mondale campaign manager Bob Beckel said their strategy was to reverse the Democrats' protest image: "In 1968 and 1972, Americans saw Democrats burning flags on television. Now they see Democrats waving them." The Reagan advance staff felt personally offended that their opposition was using symbols they believed belonged to them, so they arranged the ultimate patriotic photo-op. At a rally in Houston the following week, the advance staff spent $1,740 on flags and patriotic signs and vowed that no one would "out-patriot" Ronald Reagan.

Another popular patriotic symbol is soldiers and veterans of the armed forces. Soldiers are frequently used to make the enthymematic argument that a candidate is supported by the troops, strong on defense, or a capable commander in chief. Every president holds media events at military commencements and bases to tap into the symbolic value of men and women in uniform. For example, Reagan used the armed forces as props on countless occasions, such as his dining with the troops at the DMZ in Korea, shaking hands with cadets at the West Point Commencement, observing weapons training aboard the USS *Constellation*, saluting shipmen at the recommissioning ceremony for the USS *New Jersey*, and standing under the guns of the USS *Iowa* during the Statue of Liberty Centennial celebration. As discussed in the first chapter, media events with soldiers were also one of the favorite tropes of the George W. Bush administration.

CROWDS

One of the primary concerns of advance staffers is building and managing a large and favorable crowd. According to the Reagan advance manual, "Perhaps the most important aspect of the advanceman's job, and the most challenging, is the raising of a large and enthusiastic crowd for The President."[35] Advancemen and -women have crowd building down to a science. For instance, the Reagan advance manual has thirty pages devoted to how to build a large crowd and how to make crowds appear large in media coverage. The number of people in the crowd is very important, or more specifically, the *perception* of the crowd size trumps all. Empty seats in the audience are one of the top concerns of advance staff, as exemplified by the Nixon advance manual: "*Principle No. One of Advancing.* It is much better to stuff 6,000 people into a 5,000 person auditorium than 20,000 into a 30,000 seat auditorium, because if the press sees empty seats, instead of saying 20,000 people showed up they will say that 10,000 didn't."[36] A huge crowd is beneficial, but it is more important that the hall is filled, that people were waiting outside trying to get in, and that the press captured it all. The advance staff's goal is always to support the candidate with seemingly large and supportive crowds and to have those crowds featured in media coverage of the event. An advance man wants the headline in the next day's newspaper to read, "Overflow Crowd Turns Out to Hear Candidate."

Advancemen and women think of the immediate audience in the hall only as a prop for the larger audience watching the event on television or reading about it online or in a newspaper. This is not hidden in the advance manuals, for example, George H. W. Bush's manual clearly spells this out: "Don't forget this central point: The crowd is merely a backdrop for the media reports."[37] Advance staffers move the crowd just as they would move a banner or flag. The same Nixon manual explains this point: "Where the Advanceman wants spectators to stand and where the spectators themselves want to stand do not necessarily coincide. Spectators like to stand where they can see. From the Advanceman's point of view, this is an absurd notion. They should stand where they can fill space and make the area look crowded for the benefit of TV and press cameramen."[38]

Successful crowd development provides two important symbolic functions at a media event: to demonstrate popularity and to establish widespread and diverse support and momentum. For instance, if an event or rally was overflowing with people, advancemen argue, the media would be more likely to report that the candidate was popular and had momentum for his presidency and policies. Pictures of a candidate juxtaposed with cheering supporters, packed speech halls, and autograph seekers act as a visual "social proof"—that what is popular must be good.[39] Looking again at Reagan's whistle-stop tour through Ohio in the 1984 presidential campaign, huge crowds were built and used to show that Reagan was still a very popular president, even as he was slumping after the first presidential debate. Attempts were also made to draw a diverse crowd to argue that Reagan was supported by Americans of various social and economic backgrounds. The efforts of the advance staff were successful because in media coverage of the events, reporters frequently mentioned that Reagan drew large and diverse crowds. Steven Weisman described the "enormous, exuberant crowds" in his piece for the *New York Times*,

> Along the route there were clusters of cheering onlookers, sometimes in the hundreds and even thousands—factory workers in overalls and hard hats, high school bands and children waving flags, farmers in overalls standing on top of flatbed trucks, mothers hoisting small children to their shoulders and taking pictures, families sitting in lawn chairs with their dogs barking, and most everybody waving and smiling.[40]

In their television coverage, all three networks also showed multiple pictures of cheering crowds, with CBS noting that Reagan drew "huge crowds"[41] and NBC reporting that "crowds were big all day."[42] Not only did these crowds illustrate that Reagan was popular, they also offered a type of social proof for Reagan's policies and candidacy. Even if a reporter was to describe the opposing viewpoint to the president's views, Reagan was visually portrayed as well-liked by the American people. Based on the visual arguments forwarded by these advanced crowds, it was difficult to conclude anything besides Reagan was a popular commander-in-chief. Barack Obama and Joe Biden made a similar train trip to Washington, DC for their 2009 inauguration and received glowing media coverage as well.

Large crowds are not natural occurrences; they are planned and orchestrated—anytime you see a large crowd, be it political rally or protest, there will be advance staff off camera coordinating the show. There are several tactics advancemen use to build crowds, depending on the nature of the event. Of course, the event must be publicized using every avenue possible—using press releases to get free coverage in the press, placing announcements on Internet websites, sending e-mails or setting up telephone backs to contact supporters, leafleting, and placing posters around town. To maximize publicity, details of the trip and schedule are released bit by bit in varying formats and through various spokespeople; first a local party leader will hold a press conference announcing the trip, then a different surrogate gives interviews with times and locations of events, and so on. No avenue for recruiting audiences is ignored. To build interest on talk radio, workers or volunteers can call the station and say they heard a rumor that the candidate might speak and ask for more details, while other workers call in with details of the event and statements of support for the candidate. To encourage attendance at an event, tickets can be distributed even when tickets are not necessary or required for admittance. A common rule of thumb is to give out at least double the number of tickets as the venue can hold. Groups with strong memberships are also invited, such as labor unions, civic associations, churches, senior groups, convention bureaus, and Chambers of Commerce. Group invitations can also be sent to elementary, middle, and high schools to encourage schools to close school for the day or bus their students to the event. One reason high school bands are excellent for events is that in addition to the entertainment and local color that they provide, is that they also bring parents and grandparents who want to see their son or daughter play in this historic campaign event. Local or national celebrities can do wonders for crowd building. In the 2008 Republican primaries, Mike Huckabee traveled with action movie star Chuck Norris, which raised his profile among likely voters and the media and brought bodies to his events. Another tactic is to hold events in venues with built-in crowds where people naturally gather such as shopping malls and farmers markets—people attract people and once you have a mass of people it becomes easier to use word of mouth to create a truly large event.

Ideally event locations should be scalable—that is, the hall or arena begins as a small space and as more crowds appear for the event, moveable walls can be opened or curtains can be drawn to vary the size of the rally. John Kerry used this strategy in a 2004 rally in Madison, Wisconsin, 5 days before the November Election. The advance staff wanted a huge event to show momentum and support for the Democratic challenger so they chose to hold the event on a street near the state capitol. Streets are always a challenge for crowd builders because it is challenging to recruit the tens of thousands needed to truly fill the space. The Kerry team solved this problem by setting up a huge billboard reading "Wisconsin is Kerry Country" on wheels in the street opposite the stage that could be rolled back as the crowd grew larger to ensure the street always looked full. As a safety measure, Kerry was introduced by Bruce Springsteen who was sure to bring a crowd in this Kerry-leaning college town. So media cameras could fully depict the enormity of the crowd, the Kerry staff placed a large construction lift behind the podium which photographers and video shooters could use to get an overhead shot of the cheering supporters and the celebratory candidate.

After an enthusiastic and large crowd has been built, the advance staff must take steps to encourage the media to show images of the crowd and discuss it as part of their stories. One technique used by Reagan's advance office was to cut a small hole in the backdrop behind Reagan. During the event, the advance staff would rotate reporters and photographers into that hole so they could get a reverse "over the shoulder shot" of Reagan. This "over the shoulder shot" made Reagan appear very close to the crowd and communicated the size, excitement, and diversity of the crowd by showing their faces. This technique was used frequently in the

1984 campaign, and many photographs in *Time* and *Newsweek* from that year have the imprint of an advance staffer cutting a hole in the backdrop.[43] Similarly the advance team will work with a supportive local officeholder, such as a chief of police, to provide a favorable estimate of the size of the crowd. The LBJ advance manual implies the importance of working with a sympathetic local: "A proper crowd estimator such as the chief of police or the mayor should be selected and well briefed before the occasion so that he is prepared to give a proper estimate of the size of the crowd. This man should be kept close at hand when the Presidential part arrives so that his figure might be checked with the White House staff and if proper then be given over to the press office."[44] Of course, keeping this official close will allow the campaign to pressure them to increase their estimate.

To ensure that the crowd will be supportive, advance staff will plant cheerleaders throughout the crowd to stoke enthusiasm and make certain that the crowd reacts with uproarious applause at the right moments in the speech. In a tradition going back to claques—a group of professional applauders used in French opera houses and theatres—advancemen use these volunteers to build passion in the crowd and give the impression of widespread support for the candidate and his policies. As the Carter advance manual describes: "Plan in advance to sprinkle your crowd with cheerleaders and claques. They must start clapping, chants, or cheers, and even songs when the Candidate arrives and after appropriate lines during his moving through a crowd and/or speech."[45] The LBJ advance office had a similar directive: "At least 100 people should be scattered throughout the audience as leaders of applause. They should be instructed to forthrightly start the applause at appropriate times. Applause in all instances should begin with the President's last words and there should not be a pause between the end of a sentence and the beginning of the applause."[46] Psychologist Robert Cialdini explains how audiences look to others to decide what constitutes appropriate behavior: "One means we use to determine what is correct is to find out what other people think is correct."[47] At media events, what is correct is the candidate and the appropriate behavior is to cheer the candidate and his policies. Everything in an event must be planned and controlled, and these cheerleaders allow the advance staff to manage the crowd reaction. As the Nixon advance manual states: "You should always have a program to build-up audience enthusiasm ahead of time. You should have a plan for doing this and should make sure that it's carried out so that it's not left up to the local people to have it done."[48]

Just as crowd enthusiasm is orchestrated, it is also standard practice in most campaigns to plant questions with audience members in a town hall event where the candidate may take questions. Anytime a candidate opens up an event for questions, they lose some control and risk the event going "off message" as audience members inquire about their own personal issues. While not every question is planned, enough questions must be prearranged to guarantee that the necessary sound bite on the day's theme is captured on the television cameras at the back of the room. To avoid negative publicity, this works best when questions are given to known supporters who would not admit to asking a leading question and would be flattered to be asking the candidate a question. Hillary Clinton's campaign learned this lesson in Iowa in the 2008 presidential caucus.[49] At a town hall event at a biodiesel plant in Newton, Iowa, a Clinton staffer approached a college student and gave her a preprinted question labeled "[college student]" about global warming. When Clinton called on the young women, it was obvious she was prepared to answer the rehearsed question as Clinton replied, "You know, I find as I travel around Iowa that it's usually young people that ask me about global warming."[50] Later, the student regretted her participation in the made-for-television exchange and told her story in her college newspaper. When the story was picked up in the national media, it resulted in several days of negative stories about the authenticity of Clinton's candidacy. George W. Bush's administration frequently used this tactic in their town halls and issue panels. Anyone who would share the stage and microphone with the president was hand-picked to support the president's message and was extensively prepped and rehearsed with staffers dismissing potential participants who went off-message.[51] In an October 13, 2005, event billed as a question-and-answer session allowing President Bush to question and hear directly from soldiers in Iraq, the television feed was inadvertently broadcast early and showed an elaborate rehearsal of the president's prepared questions and the soldiers memorized, scripted, and coached answers.[52] In an extreme example broadcast on Fox News, MSNBC, and other outlets, officials from the Federal Emergency Management Agency faked a press conference with FEMA public affairs staff playing the part of journalists and throwing softball questions to the deputy administrator of FEMA.[53]

Even with this planning, the crowd can also be a distraction to a candidate's message if protestors or demonstrators disrupt the event, and detecting and removing hecklers is a main concern during the event. Every advance manual has sections on dealing with demonstrators, and there are two primary strategies for dealing with protestors. The first tactic is to attempt to prevent them from entering your event. According to Nixon advanceman Charles Stuart, during the 1968 campaign when a hippy-looking young man and woman would attempt to enter a presidential rally, ticket-takers would tell them their tickets were counterfeit and that they couldn't be admitted to the event.[54] They would then be directed to an office several blocks away to get replacement tickets, and when they would arrive at the office they would be told that all the tickets had been distributed, but that more would be arriving shortly. Obviously, additional tickets would never arrive. The second Bush administration was notorious for protecting their tickets. Instead of flooding an area with tickets, they would only distribute them through Republican and pro-administration groups in an attempt to ensure a favorable audience. Only those with special VIP tickets, which the Bush advance manual emphasizes should only be given to groups "*extremely* supportive of the President," could sit behind the president on stage or on the floor between the camera platforms and the speaker. Notably, the ACLU filed a lawsuit against Greg Jenkins, former Director of White House Presidential Advance under Bush for this strategy on behalf of two plaintiffs who were arrested for wearing T-shirts critical of the president and two who where removed from a town hall meeting because they had an antiwar bumper sticker on their car. The second tactic is to use intimidation and force to silence the protestors or remove them from the hall. Both parties place "etiquette squads," "rally squads," or using the more cynical term—"goon squads," throughout the crowd to surround and possibly escort unruly audience members out of the hall. These supporters are taught to surround protestors with large signs so that other audience members, or more importantly the cameras on the media platform, will not see the demonstration and drown out the hecklers by chanting "USA! USA! USA!" If possible, it is preferred to let the favorable crowd react and regulate protestors and not give the demonstrators credibility by officially responding.

SIGNS AND BANNERS

A more direct method to support the candidate's message in an event is through the use of signs and banners. Depending on the objective of the event, signs are produced to be hung behind the candidate, hand-painted signs are distributed to audience members in front of the podium, or large banners are suspended from buildings or trucks. Reagan image maker Michael Deaver illustrates the importance of signs, writing, "My standing joke with Bill Henkel, the head of the advance team, was: If you can't give me a good visual, give me a big sign."[55] Signs and banners have two functions for an event: to make the event more mediagenic and to reinforce the candidate's message through text or visual symbols. Signs and banners are designed to add color to an event and reinforce the candidate's message in media coverage of the event. Since the advance staff largely controls the media vantage points, they are able to predict and stage the backdrops that will appear in images of the president from the designated press areas. Backdrops are planned for the wide establishing shot, the more narrow head shot, the cut-away shot from the side, and the shot from the "chute" in front of the podium. For each of these shots, a different background is created to reinforce the message of the event. For instance, at a Reagan-Bush rally during the 1984 campaign, the advance staff planned for both the straight-on shot and the cut away shot. In the wide, straight-on shot the banner read, "Leadership TEXANS can trust," while in the closer, cut-away shot news cameras captured a picture of the president with the word "Leadership" over his shoulder. It has become commonplace to use repetitive "message of the day" banners as backdrops behind the lectern, so that speaker's verbal message will be reinforced with the written message in the close-up talking head shot. So in an event on the economy, the backdrop behind the candidate will read "Working for American Jobs" or "Strengthening our Economic Future." Even if the viewer at home has their television volume muted, they will understand the desired message communicated by the event.

Signs can be placed anywhere they will be seen by photographers. Advance staffers are limited only by their creativity. The Kerry advance staff in the 2004 campaign began hanging signs and huge American flags at an angle from the ceiling to the back wall behind the candidate so photographers shooting up from the area in front of the podium toward the speaking candidate would get the sign or flag in the shot. It has become commonplace to also place signs on the floor of the speaking platform, especially during town hall events, so that photographers shooting from above will see the sign under the candidate's feet. Even if the event is outdoors, that will not prevent the hanging of a good sign—signs can be strung between two cranes or construction lifts, hung from trees, or suspended from balloons on a calm day.

There are two basic types of signs, professionally printed banners and handmade placards, and advance manuals provide very specific guidelines for preparing both. For example, for professional printed banners, George H. W. Bush's advance staff is directed to only use framed banners that range in size from 4' × 16' to 4' × 20' with a nonreflective dark background and light contrasting colors for lettering.[56] Advance manuals give even more information about how to create handmade looking signs. "A great deal of effort should go into the making of homemade signs, banners and the like. There can never be too many of these. ten thousand homemade signs should be a minimum goal at any Presidential appearance. They should be colorful, different and attractive," reads the LBJ advance manual.[57] Hand-painted signs are created by the advance staff before an event and distributed to the audience to give the impression that the audience made their own signs and brought them to the event. The trick is to create signs that are professional enough to be read and just amateur enough so that television viewers would assume the audience made the signs at home in support of the candidate. You can always tell the difference between handmade signs made by the campaign and genuine signs brought to the event by the audience, because genuine signs have a message written on only one side of the poster while campaign-created signs are double-sided. During the event, the audience member will want to show their sign to the candidate, and if the poster is one-sided, the cameras on the media platform at the rear of the room will capture a room filled with blank signs, so advance people have learned to paint both sides of signs. In the 2008 presidential campaign, when John McCain would appear at rallies with his "every man" surrogate Joe the Plumber, McCain's advance staff would fill the crowds with signs of popular professions, such as "I'm Joe the teacher" and "I am Joe the nurse" to appeal to these working class groups.

SETTING AND BACKDROP

The setting and symbolic trappings for a speech are just as important, if not more important than the words the candidate speaks. This fact was not lost on Fred Dutton, Deputy National Chairman for Lyndon Johnson's 1964 campaign. In a September 28, 1964, memo about possible speech themes to Bill Moyers, special assistant to President Lyndon Johnson, Dutton argues: "I believe that the speech texts are no more important . . . perhaps not as important . . . in a campaign sense as the 'situations' in which the President appears during October: the backgrounds, the people he is with and, most important, the actions he takes. His schedule should be constructed that these latter considerations are given full weight."[58] Dutton then gives Moyers a list of possible situations the president should consider, such as meeting with FBI Director J. Edgar Hoover to demonstrate commitment to "the law and order" issue, using the Johnson family to "show him off well as a family man and blunt the politician-image," and the inclusion of prominent women in "picture situations, television appearances, platform groups, and similar situations."

Advancemen and -women have traditionally relied on velour curtains, typically in a dark blue color known as "presidential blue," to provide a stately backdrop and block unsightly areas of meeting rooms, halls, and gymnasiums. However, other backdrops and settings can be used to tell the story of the event and drive the news narrative through setting and background. Again, the Reagan advance manual provides an explanation of how they used setting to communicate a message:

> A ten-foot high Royal blue backdrop is traditionally used, but don't limit yourself to just a traditional backdrop. Imagination is the key. For example, a backdrop of hay for a farm rally, a backdrop of Boy Scouts for a civic rally, or a backdrop of a dozen American flags or a huge American flag for a patriotic event. In setting your backdrop, remember that the backdrop should always send a message within the photograph.[59]

These backdrops and settings establish the tone and mood of an event, what advance people call "atmosphere." A candidate could illustrate his support for medical research by looking at a computer screen or talking to a group of scientists; he could highlight his belief in and support for education by reading to children; or, he could strengthen his image among values voters by going to church and making an "unscheduled" stop by the Vietnam Memorial one Sunday. A memo from Nixon's chief of staff H. R. Haldeman and scheduling director Dwight Chapin directs the advance staff to surround the president with police officers: "We've got to look for more opportunities for pictures of the President with policemen, not just troops lined up to be thanked for motorcycle escorts, but good informal shots chatting with policemen on a friendly basis, showing rapport, etc."[60]

Another popular backdrop is to place supporters on the rostrum behind the candidate or to place the candidate in the round to show their closeness to voters. For example, for the final night of the 2004 Republican Convention in New York City, Madison Square Garden was redesigned with a small stage in the center of the convention floor such that President Bush would speak in the round— surrounded by adoring supporters like a political gladiator in the center of a modern, mediated coliseum. The supporters are carefully selected to communicate the candidate's message and reinforce the verbal message of the speech: factory workers are placed behind the politician for an economic speech, nurses for healthcare, teachers for education, and so on. Typically, when the crowd is building, a volunteer is given a list of demographics and asked to find enthusiastic audience members who fit that profile.

Crowds can be used to communicate a message visually that could never be stated verbally. When questions where raised about Barack Obama's ability to connect with white voters in the 2008 Democratic North Carolina primary, he delivered his victory speech in front of a group of middle-class white women, and when John McCain campaigned in New Hampshire, Hispanic audience members where asked to stand behind the candidate to add "diversity" to the crowd.[61] The Obama campaign was hit with several negative headlines from using this tactic. At a rally for Michelle Obama at Carnegie Mellon University, a staffer who was carefully arranging the crowd behind the podium moved an Asian student off camera and was overhead saying, "Get me more white people, we need more white people."[62] And when planning two events in Detroit, Michigan, Muslim audience members were barred from sitting near the candidate because they were wearing headscarves with one volunteer explaining that it is not good for Muslim Americans to be seen on television or associated with Obama.[63]

Black Advance

Advance staffers must always be aware of so-called black advance, an attempt by your opponent to infiltrate your event or staff and sabotage your rally. Black advance usually takes the form of planting detractors in the audience to boo or ask negative questions, spreading misinformation about the details of a rally to confuse and frustrate the audience such as hanging posters that misstate the time or location of an event, or holding negative signs along a parade route. In one notable case of black advance in the 2004 Indiana Democratic primary, a representative for Barack Obama's campaign attended a speech to students by Bill Clinton at Indiana University and handed out free tickets to a Dave Matthews concert causing a large percentage of the crowd to leave the event and wait in line for the concert tickets.

Perhaps the most famous blackadvance man is Democratic prankster Dick Tuck.[64] Advance lore has it that Tuck was working for Congresswoman Helen Gahagan Douglas in her 1950 U.S. Senate campaign when he was a student at the University of California, Santa Barbara. A professor, who knew he was involved in politics, but didn't know his party allegiance, asked him to advance a Nixon visit. Tuck rented a huge auditorium, invited only a handful of people, and gave a sleep-inducing introduction to Nixon in which he said Nixon would speak about the International Monetary Fund, a subject outside Nixon's primary expertise. Tuck continued to be a thorn in Nixon's side throughout his political career. Greeting Nixon after the first televised debate with John Kennedy in the 1960 campaign was a Tuck plant—an elderly woman who embraced Nixon and said, "Don't worry son. Kennedy won last night but you'll do better next time." And when Nixon was delivering a whistle-stop speech aboard his campaign train, Tuck donned a railman's cap and signaled the train engineer to leave the station. At yet another event, Tuck switched the "Nixon" and "VIP" signs on two campaign buses and sent Nixon to a hotel instead of a television interview.

Counteradvance efforts are not always so creative. It is commonplace to attempt to offset the advance efforts of your opponent—a practice known as "bracketing"—by staging your own counterevents, targeting the local media using campaign surrogates, or bombarding the media with news releases refuting the frame or message of an event. Since all major campaigns have advance and media consultants, it can be assumed that every event will be countered through similar efforts by the opposing candidate. Because of this, advance staff must limit the opportunities for rebuttal and be careful not to give the opposition any "ammo" they can use in bracketing their own events.

Conclusion

One of the most important groups of staff assistants in any political campaign are the advancemen and -women. Although they are frequently overlooked, these consultants directly shape the image of the candidate by working with the news media to stage events that are favorable to the candidate. The handiwork of these behind-the-scenes warriors has a direct impact on the tenor and narrative of the campaign and is influential in shaping voter's perceptions of the candidates. As this chapter discussed, advance personnel now have a sophisticated set of event-building and media-managing tools that are consistently used because of their time-tested effectiveness. What was once considered by some to be an art has developed into a distinctive science and a full-fledged occupation for many.

Notes

1. Jerry Bruno and Jeff Greenfield, *The Advance Man* (New York: Morrow, 1971), 28.

2. For example, see Patrick S. Halley, *On the Road with Hillary: A Behind-the-Scenes Look at the Journey from Arkansas to the U.S. Senate* (New York: Viking 2002).

3. Robert Agranoff, *The Management of Election Campaigns* (Boston: Holbrook Press, 1976), 302.

4. Advance Manual, folder: Advance Manual (1), box 1, Rosenberger-Blaser Papers, Ford Library.

5. Halley, *On the Road,* 6.

6. Charles Stuart, *Never Trust a Local: Inside the Nixon White House* (New York: Algora, 2005), 15.

7. Carter/Mondale Advance Manual, folder: 1976 Presidential Campaign, box 317, Office Files of Betty Rainwater, Carter Library.

8. Advance Operations Manual, 1981, folder "Advance Office Operations Manual," box 19325, William Henkel Files, Ronald Reagan Library, 5.

9. Carter/Mondale Advance Manual, folder: Advance Manual, box 1, Jody Powell Papers, Carter Library.

10. Bill Lacy, Jim Hooley, Andrew Littlefair, and Gary Foster, *Stagecraft Stories* (Lawrence, KS: Robert Dole Institute of Politics, 2005).

11. Advanceman's Checklist 1971, folder: Advanceman's Checklist 1971, box 106, 1970 Campaign File: Dean, Nixon Presidential Materials.

12. Advance Operations Manual, Reagan Library, 17.

13. Advance Manual, folder: Advance Manual (1), box 1, Rosenberger-Blaser Papers, Ford Library.

14. Advance Operations Manual, Reagan Library, 4.

15. Advance Manual Revision, folder: Advance Manual Revision re "The Press" Ch. VIII (2), box 1, Rosenberger-Blaser Papers, Ford Library.

16. Advance Operations Manual, Reagan Library.

17. Lacy, Hooley, Littlefair, and Foster, *Stagecraft Stories.*

18. Barbara Pfetsch, "Government News Management," in *The Politics of News: The News of Politics,* ed. Doris A. Graber, Denis McQuail, and Pippa Norris (Washington, DC: CQ Press, 1998), 74–75.

19. Halley, *On the Road,* 23.

20. Advance Operations Manual, Reagan Library.

21. Memo, Haldeman to Chapin, 8 June 1969, folder: Advance Men - Resumes, box 19, WHSF: Chapin, Nixon Presidential Materials.

22. Presidential Remarks, Remarks October 12, 1984, Reagan Library.

23. Steven R. Weisman, "Reagan Follows the Tracks of Truman '48 Train Tour," *New York Times* (October 13, 1984), 9.

24. Carter/Mondale Advance Manual, folder: 1976 Presidential Campaign, box 317, Office Files of Betty Rainwater, Carter Library.

25. Presidential Advance Manual, folder: The Presidential Advance Manual 1971, box 387, WHSF: Haldeman, Nixon Presidential Materials.

26. Memo, Rafshoon to Carter, 27 September 1978, folder: 90 Day Plan - Draft, box 29, Office Files of Greg Schneider, Carter Library.

27. Memo, Rafshoon to Carter, folder: Memoranda from Jerry Rafshoon – June, July, and August, 1979, box 28, Office Files of Greg Schneider, Carter Library.

28. Advance Operations Manual, Reagan Library.

29. Presidential Advance Manual, folder: The Presidential Advance Manual 1971, box 387, WHSF: Haldeman, Nixon Presidential Materials.

30. Memo, Dutton to Moyers, 26 September 1964, folder: Campaign, box 53, Office Files of Bill Moyers, LBJ Library.

31. Carrie Budoff Brown, "Obama's Close-up Strategy," Politico.com (May 5, 2008); Christopher Cooper and Nick Timiraos, "Obama is Getting Back to Getting Close to Voters, *Wall Street Journal* (May 5, 2008), A5.

32. Charles S. Johnson, "Experts: Obama's Butte Visit a Perfect Fit," *Missoulian* (July 3, 2008).

33. Advance Operations Manual, Reagan Library, 197.

34. Martin Schram, *The Great American Video Game: Presidential Politics in the Television Age* (New York: William Morrow, 1987), 226–29.

35. Advance Operations Manual, Reagan Library.

36. Advance Manual, folder: Advance Manual (1), box 1, Rosenberger-Blaser Papers, Ford Library.

37. Advance Manual, folder: Advance Manual (1), Bush Library.

38. Advance Manual, folder: Advance Manual (1), box 1, Rosenberger-Blaser Papers, Ford Library.

39. Robert B. Cialdini, *Influence: The Psychology of Persuasion* (Rev. ed.) (New York: Morrow, 1993).

40. Weisman, "Reagan Follows," 9.

41. Dan Rather, Bruce Morton, Lesley Stahl, and Bill Plante, "Campaign 1984/debate," *CBS Evening News* (October 12, 1984). Available at http://tvnews.vanderbilt.edu.

42. Tom Brokaw, Roger Mudd, and Chris Wallace, "Decision 1984/debate," *NBC Evening News* (October 12, 1984). Available at http://tvnews.vanderbilt.edu.

43. Lacy, Hooley, Littlefair, and Foster, *Stagecraft Stories.*

44. Presidential Advance Checklist, folder: Advance Men, box 1, Office Files of James R. Jones, LBJ Library.

45. Carter/Mondale Advance Manual, folder: Advance Manual, box 1, Jody Powell Papers, Carter Library.

46. Presidential Advance Checklist, folder: Advance Men, box 1, Office Files of James R. Jones, LBJ Library.

47. Cialdini, *Influence,* 116.

48. Presidential Advance Manual, folder: The Presidential Advance Manual 1971, box 387, WHSF: Haldeman, Nixon Presidential Materials.

49. Andrew Malcolm, "Clinton's Planted Question in Iowa; Crowd Control," *Swamp* (November 10, 2007); Chris Welch and David Schechter, "Student Describes How She Became a Clinton Plant," CNN.com (November 13, 2007).

50. Malcolm, "Clinton's Planted Question."

51. Frank Rich, "Enron: Patron Saint of Bush's Fake News," *New York Times* (March 20, 2005).

52. Dan Froomkin, "Caught on Tape," *Washington Post* (October 14, 2005).

53. Al Kamen, "FEMA Meets the Press, which Happens to be . . . FEMA," *Washington Post* (October 26, 2007), A19.

54. Charles Stuart, *Never Trust a Local: Inside the Nixon White House* (New York: Algora, 2005), 15.

55. Michael K. Deaver and Mickey Herskowitz, *Behind the Scenes: In Which the Author Talks about Ronald and Nancy Reagan . . . and Himself* (New York: Morrow, 1987), 140.

56. Presidential Banner Guidelines, folder: American Enterprise Institute Meeting 12/4/91, Office Files of Peggy Hazelrigg, George H. W. Bush Library.

57. Presidential Advance Checklist, folder: Advance Men, box 1, Office Files of James R. Jones, LBJ Library.

58. Memo, Dutton to Moyers, 28 September 1964, folder: Campaign, box 53, Office Files of Bill Moyers, LBJ Library.

59. Advance Operations Manual, Reagan Library.

60. Memo, Haldeman to Chapin, 28 August 1970, folder: Memo from HRH Jan 1970–August 1970, box 18, WHSF: Chapin, Nixon Presidential Materials.

61. Ben Smith, "Muslims Barred from Picture at Obama Event," Politico.com (June 18, 2008).

62. Andrew Peters, "Michelle Obama Speaks at Presidential Rally in Skibo Gym," *Tartan* (April 7, 2008).

63. Smith, "Muslims Barred."

64. Paul F. Boller, *Presidential Campaigns: From George Washington to George W. Bush* (New York: Oxford University Press, 2004); Bruce L. Felknor, *Dirty Politics* (New York: Norton, 1966); Time, "The Man who Bugged Nixon," *Time* (August 13, 1973), 16–17.

CHAPTER 4

The Rhetorical Impact
of Media Events

> Pictures drowned out my words. Pictures are emotional and
> passionate and are capable of influencing viewers much
> more than mere words. We form judgments about what we
> see, and our leaders are aware of this. Visual images are
> much more powerful and remain with us longer.
>
> —Lesley Stahl, CBS News White House Correspondent[1]

This quote is veteran journalist Lesley Stahl's explanation for one of the most
repeated anecdotes about the difficulty journalists have in covering media
events—a story used so often to illustrate the complicated relationship between the president and the press that it is referred to as "Lesley's Parable."[2]
Stahl, White House correspondent for CBS during the Reagan administration,
frequently uses the story in her public speeches[3] and it appears in many analyses of news management of presidents, especially Ronald Reagan, and larger
discussions of the influence of media events and visuals in political communication.[4]

"Lesley's Parable" offers one explanation of the communication effectiveness
for a president labeled "The Great Communicator" and "The Teflon President."
Tired of being pushed and pulled by the Ronald Reagan news management operation, CBS News correspondent Lesley Stahl decided she would expose their
media manipulation tactics by running an extended, 6-minute exposé on the
Reagan administration's use of television and media events. The story Stahl produced was critical of what she believed were White House efforts to trump substance with symbolism. The piece featured Stahl's explanation of the advance

techniques used by Reagan's staff and a deconstruction of several Reagan events. The voiceover on the piece read:

> How does Ronald Reagan use television? Brilliantly. He's been criti-
> cized as the rich man's president, but the TV pictures say it isn't so.
> Mr. Reagan could have an age problem, but the TV pictures say it
> isn't so. The orchestration of television coverage absorbs the White
> House. Their goal? To emphasize the president's greatest asset, which
> his aides say is his personality. They provide pictures of him looking
> like a leader . . . confident, with his Marlboro Man walk . . . a good
> family man. Mr. Reagan tries to counter the memory of an unpopu-
> lar issue with a carefully chosen backdrop that actually contradicts
> the president's policy. . . . President Reagan is accused of running a
> campaign in which he highlights the images and hides from the is-
> sues. But there's no evidence that the charge will hurt him because
> when the people see the president on television, he makes them feel
> good: about America, about themselves, and about him.[5]

Over Stahl's critique, her producer edited in shots from Reagan media events: Reagan picnicking with ordinary folks, receiving an Olympic torch from a run-ner, talking with farmers in a field, and surrounded by American flags, brass bands, bunting, balloons, and worshipping crowds.

Stahl was worried that the negative piece might upset White House officials and result in backlash from the administration: "I knew the piece would have an impact, if only because it was so long: five minutes and 40 seconds, practically a documentary in Evening News terms. I worried that my sources in the White House would be angry enough to freeze me out."[6] Indeed, Stahl says she did re-ceive a call from Reagan advisor Dick Darman shortly after the story aired. Much to her surprise, Darman and other administration officials were not angry and to the contrary, they thanked Stahl for the piece and thought it was good for their campaign. Darman said to Stahl, "Way to go, kiddo. What a great story! We loved it."[7] Stahl recalled that she thought they were joking and asked, "Excuse me?" Darman replied, "We really loved it. Five minutes of free media. We owe you big time." Stahl asked, "Why are you so happy? Didn't you hear what I said?" Giving the punch line of the parable, Darman said to Stahl, "Nobody heard what you said. You guys in Televisionland haven't figured it out have you? When the pic-tures are powerful and emotional, they override if not completely drown out the sound. Lesley, I mean it, nobody heard you."[8] Stahl said she examined her piece again, this time with the sound off, and found that the Reagan official was right—her story had accepted the Reagan frame and was practically an unpaid political commercial—a brilliant montage of Reagan surrounded with flags, children, bal-loons, and cheering supporters. Asked if this experience changed the way she produces her stories Stahl said, "Not really. I'm still trapped, because my pieces are written to the pictures we have."[9]

"Lesley's Parable" lives on and is important for several reasons: it is about the transformation of politics and the disengagement of voters in the media age, it is an amusing story about how a gotcha journalist was trumped by the Great Communicator, it summarizes press futility during the Reagan administration, and it raises questions about the power of televised media events in political affairs.[10] The questions raised by the parable are numerous: Do images trump words as Stahl argues or do words dominate and define images? What function did they play in building a candidate's image? How does the news media cover a candidate or president who communicates via media events?

Observers who have attempted to answer these questions can be broken into two camps. The first camp, represented by Stahl, argues that the eye is more powerful than the ear in today's politics and that Reagan manipulated the media and voters by playing to the camera with media events. For example, Glenn Elert argues, "Unfortunately for the American people, in protecting his television image Reagan forgot the substance of being president,"[11] and Keith Boykin asserts, "Reagan's people knew the cliché that 'a picture is worth a thousand words.' And they knew the only three things that get covered in elections are mistakes, attacks and pictures."[12] The rival camp argues the opposite, that Reagan's power lied in his ideas and principles and his ability to verbally articulate them to the American people. Perhaps the best questioning of "Lesley's Parable" comes from noted media critic Jay Rosen: "[The] 'Nobody heard the words' [position] is spectacularly wrong about Reagan. His words, and the way they are connected, were the source of his power. The eye over the ear is wrong about Reagan. Sure he always looked good, but compared to his oratorical command, his command of imagery—and Michael Deaver's command of wizardry—are ordinary and nothing more. [The viewpoint that] the public is mesmerized by images is wrong about the public, and about Reagan. He spoke to the nation about the most basic things in politics, which are also the most profound, without going over its head."[13] Rosen's argument is that Reagan was a man of large ideas and the press was not equipped to cover those big ideas.

Lesley's parable is a perfect starting point to consider the importance and rhetorical impact of media events, popularized by Reagan. Media events are a complex communicative phenomena and one that functions on different levels to different audiences. Neither side of the images versus words debate is completely correct because media events function as a "both/and," not an "either/or." The power of media events lies in their ability to combine all communication channels in a simple, emotional, and dramatic form that is easily digestible for news and voter consumption. This chapter explores these functions and finds that events are powerful for multiple reasons: they can drive news coverage, construct political images, make visual arguments, document and authenticate, combine communication channels, dramatize policy, compel acceptance of the frame, and generate an emotional response. After addressing each of these processes, this chapter will conclude with the most politically salient question—the degree to which media events influence voters.

Media Events Drive News Coverage (Agenda Building)

Media events give candidates and campaigns the opportunity to control the news agenda by providing news outlets with attention-grabbing visuals and interesting story lines. Since television news and, increasingly, print news, has a visual imperative, candidates can greatly improve the likelihood that their message will garner coverage if they provide engaging pictures, instead of sending out a press release or holding a basic press conference in a hotel ballroom. As Berkman and Kitch observe: "With the knowledge that the press will dutifully cover and, in most cases, will report everything that the president does, it is fairly simple to engineer situations for the president to enforce the desired image."[14] If a candidate would like their environmental position to be part of the media agenda, they could stage a series of events at national forests or at superfund sites that have been cleaned up and turned into parks. For example, in the 2008 presidential campaign, after he had secured the Republican nomination, John McCain sought to take attention away from the contested Democratic primary and build awareness of his biography as a war hero and public servant. To do this, the McCain campaign held a week-long "This Is Your Life" series of biography media events the first week of April 2008 that crisscrossed the country from his Alexandria, Virginia, high school to the Naval Academy where he learned to fly to the hanger where he was welcomed home after 5 years in a Vietnamese prison. At other stops on the "Service to America" tour, McCain visited a Children's Hospital and welcomed troops home from Iraq. These events were widely covered in the media and helped keep McCain's name in the news when most attention was on the Democrats. More importantly, McCain's biography was given coverage and the tour allowed him to emphasize his military background at an early stage of the general election campaign.

In the same way, newsmakers can limit access to the president or unfavorable images to discourage the press from reporting on those issues. If an ongoing story is unfavorable, access can be controlled and constrained—events will be carefully constructed to not give the media a new sound bite or image bite to move the story forward and keep it on the agenda. When President Reagan would return to Washington by helicopter, the press corps would be allowed to photograph the event, however, Reagan would act as if the noise from the helicopter prevented him from hearing the questions being shouted at him by the press gallery and he would simply smile and wave as he walked back to the White House. In this way, Reagan would limit the press to favorable and active images of him working, yet not give them any "news" to advance the story.

This function is not limited to politicians and is applicable to nearly all political communicators. The first step in effective communication is getting the audiences attention, and powerful media events are one of the best methods to secure that attention. For example, the AIDS Memorial Quilt put a human face on the statistics about AIDS deaths and raised the public's awareness of the disease, and war protestor Cindy Sheehan did not gather substantial media coverage until she staged a media event to attract the attention of media gatekeepers—praying at the gates of President Bush's ranch and weeping by mock graves of soldiers.

Media Events Construct Political Images

Just as events allow newsmakers to push their issues into the public agenda, events also construct political images of the candidates and leaders. As Anderson and Van Winkle review: "The 'image people' work with concepts like charismatic, handsome, youthful, etc. And they strive to keep their candidate moving— through shopping centers, old-age homes, schools, etc. They utilize visual information on television to communicate this image. Television is thus conceptualized as a vehicle for bringing the voters to the candidate, where they can see and experience his glorious image."[15] Presidents hold events to build different images, depending on their communication plan. To establish his "working rancher" image, George W. Bush borrowed an event technique from Reagan and gathered brush and did farm work on his ranch in Texas. To show he was accessible to younger and minority voters, Clinton played the saxophone on the Arsenio Hall Show. To offer an alternative to the "dirty tricks" of Nixon, Carter dressed in blue jeans and was open with the press and the American people.

Memos from the presidential libraries indicated that maintaining a desired image through events is a daily concern of candidates and their advisors. Memos throughout Carter's presidency illustrate the concern over the frequency and style of Carter's appearances and how the events were diluting Carter's image and the symbolic trappings of the presidency. Early in the Carter administration, a Memo from White House Communications Director Jerry Rafshoon attempts to persuade President Carter to restrict his public events: "You are being overexposed in an area that is very dangerous. An occasional fireside chat is O.K.; biweekly press conferences, necessary; a town meeting, perhaps. But it is not necessary to have a T.V. event every few weeks just to show that you are close to the American people. And this is happening. . . . You are running the risk of boring the people and you have 3 ½ years to go."[16] In the case of Carter, his aides felt that the "home spun peanut farmer" image was right for the 1980 campaign, but insufficient for the presidency, and that his countless events diminished the stature and magnitude of the office. This position is seen again in a memo regarding what became know as the "Malaise Speech." Greg Schneiders, Deputy Assistant to the President for Communications, argues that President Carter must change his style and tone to foster confidence among the citizenry. Schneiders writes,

> People listen to Presidential speeches the way they listen to rock music. If they heard the same speech a hundred times they still wouldn't know any of the words. But they "receive" the tone, the beat, the rhythm. Therefore, the model for this speech should be FDR's first fireside chat. Short. Action-oriented. Recognizing the seriousness of the problem but giving hope, proving leadership, inspiring confidence. The President should be terse. He should close with a couple of paragraphs about America's ability to solve our problems. He should be positive. He should not ramble on about the problems. He should not seem unsure. He should not be negative. People are turning to Kennedy or Connally because they seem attuned to the crisis of confidence in the country—they're turning to them because they look like the solution to the crisis. Jimmy Carter has to start acting like and looking like the solution. He's been describing—and bemoaning—the problem for three years now. It's time for action and the action better be big or bold.[17]

While Carter may not have taken his advice, these memos help explain how the style, setting, and language of media events builds a president's image, both favorably and unfavorably.

Another telling historical example of the image-building power of media events comes from Lyndon Johnson's presidential campaign. In the fall of 1964, many areas of the south were upset over the passage of the Civil Rights Act, which outlawed segregation in schools, public places, and employment, and many white Southern Democrats threatened to leave the Democratic Party and support Republican candidate Barry Goldwater. It was thought too dangerous (and not politically expedient) for President Johnson to visit the states to build his image and instead, first lady and southerner Lady Bird made the trip through eight southern states to stump for Johnson aboard a train dubbed *The Lady Bird*

Special. The 4-day trip from October 6 to October 9 traveled 1,628 miles and stopped in over forty cities, with rallies and speeches at each train depot. As documented in extensive clips in the LBJ library, the event was a tremendous success in attracting both audiences and favorable media coverage in local and state newspapers. the *Richmond Times-Dispatch* headlines read "Ovation Here" and "35,000 Persons Greet First Lady in Virginia," North Carolina's *News and Observer* reports that Lady Bird received a "joyous welcome" and drew "a big crowd in Ashoskie," and the *Charlotte News* declares "25,000 at the square: Happy throng hails 1st lady at Midtown," each with several front-page images of large crowds surrounding the First Lady while she speaks from the back of the train.[18] While it was only a contributing factor, Johnson did unexpectedly well in the south, winning Virginia, North Carolina, and Florida. Of course, all contemporary first ladies have frequently relied on media events to make news and promote the president and their own image and issues. Since the norms and customs of the office prevent presidential spouses from holding news conferences or giving policy speeches, they must rely on issue, formal, and ceremonial events.

Media Events Make Visual Arguments

One of the primary ways citizens learn about their leaders is through the pictures created in media events which are broadcast on television, printed in newspapers and magazines, and transmitted on the Internet. Pictures provide heuristic cues regarding the candidate's background, personality, and demeanor, and directly shape a candidate's image. Components of the picture such as selection, lighting, proximity, and setting function as visual indicators for viewers.[19] Graber explains the meanings communicated by visuals:

> When photographed from a low angle, people are judged to be taller and more powerful than when the camera looks down on them. . . . Extreme angles tend to produce negative evaluations. People tend to be evaluated more favorably when they are photographed in motion rather than in stationary positions. The closer the camera, the more people like what the candidate says. Close-ups also make people seem friendlier and more approachable. . . . Forceful hand gestures during a speech give the impression of strength and passion. . . . The background of the candidates, including color and lighting, also alters the images and moods that are conveyed.[20]

As Pulitzer Prize–winning media critic David Shaw has observed, "Clear, dramatic pictures are the key to both 'good television' and to the impact given story will have on viewers,"[21] and events are used to provide these pictures.

Since candidates have a limited amount of time to reach voters on television news, candidates attempt to pack in as many favorable symbols, both verbal and visual into their sound and image bites. As detailed in the previous chapter, elements of an image bite include the candidates dress and facial expression, camera angle, lighting, camera movement, backdrop, and other elements in the visual frame. Events are structured so photographers and videographers are limited to specific shots chosen by the campaign that achieve the campaign's objectives. Politicians cannot control the media's specific coverage decisions, but they can largely control how a message is presented visually in their events, and journalists are similarly looking to bring viewers dramatic, compelling, and evocative images.[22] Hillary Clinton media advisor Patrick Halley described the role of visuals in media events: "Ours is a very visual business, and it's driven by the television set, the most powerful weapon in politics. As a result, no politician worth her salt ever stands behind a podium and talks about the need to stimulate economic development. She goes to the gate of the closed factory and addresses a crowd of union workers who have lost their jobs. You use the visual imagery to tell the story and get the point across."[23]

Candidates and their consultants like Halley understand the importance of a good picture and a powerful image. Candidates think visually and strategically construct events to create the most powerful pictures that support the politician's goals, whether that is to get on the nightly news or appear as a strong leader.[24] In advertisements, speeches, press conferences, and other forms of communication, every visual element is carefully managed.[25] Recounting the Reagan administration's visual image management, Donald Regan wrote, "Every moment of every public appearance was scheduled, every word was scripted, every place where Reagan was expected to stand was chalked with toe marks. The President was always being prepared for a performance."[26] Popular campaigning publications such as *Campaigns and Elections* magazine instruct candidates as to what color of clothing they should wear and with whom to be photographed in their appearances.[27] Such advice suggests, "for your 'candidate with the people' shots, choose individuals who best reflect the demographic make-up of your district, with proper ethnic diversity."[28] Another asserts, "The presence of persons and objects within the frame of the image can project symbolic ideas, themes, or emotions onto candidates" such as "the American flag (patriotism), a factory production line (jobs), computers (high-tech), schoolchildren (education), and so on."[29] Perhaps Michael Deaver, visual image maker for Reagan, said it best in his book: "You get only forty to eighty seconds on any given night on the network news, and unless you can find a visual that explains your message you can't make it stick. VISUALS. I am sure the purists, who want their news unfiltered and their heroes unrehearsed, gag on the word visuals. But in the Television Age, it hasn't happened, or at least it hasn't registered, if people can't see what you see."[30] Since Deaver's time in the west wing, the 40 to 80 seconds has shrunk to less than 10 seconds, accentuating the importance of visuals created through events.

Media Events Document and Authenticate

A special type of argument made through media events is an authenticity argument. Media events excel at documenting that an event occurred and authenticating the claims and images of a leader. In a political age when consultants frequent cite "authenticity" as a fundamental ingredient in a successful candidate, events can be used to establish this genuineness and visually prove the legitimacy of a political image. Events situate presidents and candidates in meaning-filled contexts—whether those contexts are in the Oval Office, working a crowd, or traveling outside Washington. In an effort to refute the Watergate issue and re-build Nixon's eroding image, Nixon advisors planned several events to use this strategy to build his credibility and place Nixon in a context of "humanness" and "openness." Scheduling philosophy is addressed in a memo to chief of staff Alexander Haig:

> We want to personify the President's firm leadership so that the American public will come away with the thought that there is a firm hand at the helm. In an effort to have this "humanness" come through and show compassion, we should associate the President in many instances with children, a recommendation in this area is to have him visit the National Zoo on a Saturday afternoon to see the Panda bears. To go along with the openness, we should be doing more trips, more events covered by TV, and more press conferences, and more bi-partisan things. This almost gets us back into a campaign environment.[31]

In this case, we see the Nixon staff scripting events to establish Nixon's down-to-earth personality and attempting to authenticate his preferred image at a time when his image was under attack.

So called "fact-finding trips" are one example of candidates and politicians attempting to document their work to voters. During a natural disaster or political crisis, it has become commonplace for a president to travel to the region to meet with survivors and survey the damage. A president could easily learn this information from his advisors, however, that would not document his concern for those in distress nor advance the argument that the president is in touch with the country's problems. Similar fact-finding trips to war zones are held to establish that the commander in chief is informed on the conflict. Presidential candidates rely on these trips to "act presidential" on the world stage and perform the role of president. Notably, in July 2008, Barack Obama staged a multi-day international tour of Europe and the Middle East, in which he met with U.S. soldiers and foreign leaders, including President Hamid Karzai of Afghanistan, Prime Minister Nouri al-Maliki of Iraq, King Hussein of Jordan, Palestinian president Mahmoud Abbas, prime minister of Israel Ehud Olmert, Chancellor Angela Merkel of Germany, President Nicolas Sarkozy of France, and Prime Minister Gordon Brown of the United Kingdom. In the widespread media coverage of the trip, press accounts detailed Obama's attempts to "bolster his national security credentials" via media event. Events such as Obama's allow candidates to enact the presidency, and correspondingly allow voters to visualize the candidate performing the symbolic elements of the office.

Presidents take great risk in not staging these fact-finding media events in times of national crisis. In one of the few stumbles by George W. Bush's media event operation, Bush's initial response to Hurricane Katrina in Louisiana and Mississippi was not a fact-finding trip to the region, but a fly-by event aboard Air Force One in which journalists photographed the president looking out the small airplane window at the catastrophic damage. Instead of sending the message that Bush was engaged and responding to the crisis, this event had the opposite outcome and fed into the media and public frame of an out-of-touch president watching from his perch while Americans suffered. Bush's team responded to the unfavorable coverage the only way possible—by staging a series of media events over the following days challenging this negative frame.

Another standard media event which advance planners frequently use to document that politicians are in touch with working-class Americans is to visit a pub and share a drink with the bar patrons. Ronald Reagan relied on this technique to reach out to union members who traditionally voted for Democrats, but who came to the polls in large numbers for him. This strategy can backfire when events clash with the pre-existing images voters' hold of a candidate, which only serve to document the foolishness and dishonesty of a candidate. For example, in the 2008 Democratic primary, Barack Obama and Hillary Clinton both attempted this event in the same week, sharing shots and pints with "working stiffs." The resulting images looked absurd and dishonest and while the events were covered, the press largely mocked and ridiculed the candidates.

Media Events Combine All Communication Channels

The debate over Lesley Stahl's parable—was Reagan successful because of his ability to communicate the issues or did Reagan thrive because his image trumped his policy—is a false bifurcation of the issue. Reagan succeeded unlike other newsmakers because he mastered both words *and* pictures and the unique properties and functions of his media events allowed Reagan to reinforce his words with pictures, and vice versa. Reagan's masterfully written words were critically important, but equally significant were the settings, backdrops, and visuals staged by his advance staff. That is, Reagan's words were most powerful when put in the context of a well-designed media event, and Reagan was most persuasive when he communicated across multiple channels using both words and pictures. This supports the argument made by Schmuhl that what made Reagan different from other presidents was that he used television to combine the rhetorical techniques of both the pulpit and the stage "to cover all the different possibilities (persuasion, exhortation, education, leadership, entertainment) simultaneously."[32] In his media events, Reagan offered both style and substance, both a vision based on broad American themes and a moderate policy position.

Media events give candidates and politicians the tools to simultaneously communicate using multiple channels—the spoken, visual, aural, and visceral. Diverse political audiences have different learning styles and widely disparate understandings of political affairs, so the more messages a politician can incorporate into their events, the more they can communicate. The common definition of media events as shallow and deceptive "pseudo-events" is limiting and simply not true. Because of their multi-channeled nature, media events allow political communicators to imbue their messages with nuance and meaning in ways words and pictures alone cannot. When well constructed, events unite the image and the issues—the sizzle and the steak—and have an amplification effect. Visual symbols and other heuristic cues can grab the audience's attention and offer image-building cues, while spoken remarks serve an agenda-building function for media gatekeepers and opinion leaders. Media events give newsmakers multiple channels and levels of meaning, which could be understood individually or in unison, in order to appeal to diverse audiences.

Media Events Dramatize Policy

The nature of media events allows candidates and other political participants to give life to a policy and demonstrate its importance through enactment. Politicians frequently stage media events to dramatize their policies and tell stories through events to increase the likelihood that the press will cover the event. So if a candidate wants to discuss the economy, he will meet with workers at a job site, if he wants to emphasize his environmental program, he will tour a wind energy farm, and if his message of the day is education, he will visit a head start program benefiting underprivileged children. For example, when Reagan spoke next to the Brandenburg Gate on the Berlin Wall, it allowed him to visually present his strong commitment to fighting communism. Presidents will often open up cabinet meetings to the press when they want to communicate to the American people that they are working to solve the nation's problems. A political event has not happened until there are pictures of the event broadcast on television, so politicians must provide those pictures by dramatizing their positions in media events.

Television news requires interesting and compelling visuals, so it is necessary for newsmakers to make use of this function if they want to receive exposure. Without dramatic and compelling images, there will be no story and the event will not be covered. International summits and negotiations are one such news event that is typically difficult to cover until the advance staff does their work and turns the event into a media event. To feed the press their needed pictures, hand-shaking and back-patting photograph sessions are staged for cameras to communicate alliances or peaceful talks.

Media Events Compel Acceptance of the Frame

The overarching benefit of media events, in the minds of the candidates and their advance staff, is the ability to control situations and imbed every element of an event with their desired frame. For example, if the desired frame of an event is "change," the candidate's words will repeatedly emphasize change, banners and signs on the backdrop, podium, and the crowd will read "change," the crowd will be primed to chant "change," "change," "change," surrogates will be given talking points instructing them to highlight "change" in their interviews with journalists, and on and on. So if journalists wish to cover the event (and most are required by their editors to report on every event), they are forced to broadcast the candidate's frame—it is incredibly difficult, if not impossible to report on the event without publicizing the message. And even if a journalist wanted to reframe the event, they would need to find their own visuals and interviews, which is difficult to accomplish when on deadline before the campaign bus leaves for the next event. Typically, the 24/7 media is more concerned with logistics—"getting the shot"—than interpreting and contextualizing events for viewers and readers.

Influential Reagan advisor Michael Deaver provides a telling anecdote illustrating how politicians use media events to frame an issue for the press and voters:

> When we were going to make an announcement about the placing of a major order for the B-1 bomber, in the early stages of the 1984 campaign, some people close to the president were paranoid over the prospect that Walter Mondale might use this to raise the war and

peace issue. But the B-1 bomber had another potential: It meant forty thousand jobs to California. The decision was made. I wanted the president to be photographed standing next to a B-1 bomber, and I wanted a sign so big you could barely see the aircraft. The sign said: PREPARED FOR PEACE.[33]

So in this case, careful advancing by Deaver and his colleagues allowed Reagan to announce and promote the airplane order as benefiting jobs, and at the same time frame the event as "peace through strength" to inoculate against the Mondale argument.

A more recent exemplar of this function occurred at the conclusion of the 2008 Democratic Primary. After a lengthy and often contentious primary, Barack Obama and Hillary Clinton choreographed an event to demonstrate that the once rival candidates were now unified for a Democratic victory in the general election and to argue that all Democrats should come together in support of Obama. Every aspect of the event was scripted to communicate this message down to the smallest detail. Their remarks stressed how happy both candidates were to be sharing the stage and supporting each other. Obama's blue tie was color-matched to Clinton's blue pantsuit. Massive letters hung near the stage visually spelled out the theme—U–N–I–T–Y—and a second giant blue banner read "Unite for Change." On the way from Washington to the event, the candidates sat in adjoining seats on the campaign plane and smiled and chatted for the news cameras documenting their every move. In case the message was still not blatantly obvious, the event itself was held in Unity, New Hampshire—chosen both for its symbolic name and for the fact that both candidates received 107 votes from the townspeople in the state's primary. Media coverage of the event repeated and reinforced the unity message—in both words and pictures—because it was unfeasible to report on the event without publicizing the message. For example, the lead paragraph of the *New York Times* story on the event read: "UNITY, N.H.—Senators Barack Obama and Hillary Rodham Clinton set off on their maiden political voyage on Friday, trading their rivalry from the presidential primary battle for a newfound display of harmony intended to set a fresh tone for any Democrats still harboring bitterness from their grueling duel."[34] The headlines, pictures, and stories of the rally appeared to have been written by the Obama advance staff, and because the event was so carefully married to the message, in effect, they *were* written by the Obama campaign.

Even though these images are staged, they are still effective because frames made by visuals are held to less stricter standards of accountability than verbal claims.[35] And when images and words are in conflict, audiences are more likely to accept the visual than the aural or written. According to Schmuhl, "We tend to believe what we see—which is the main reason television news has higher credibility than other sources—and engaging visuals carry their own meanings, frequently quite distinct from the words we might hear. The eye overrides the ear. If there is conflict between what we are shown and what we are told, a high percentage of the viewing audience will not analyze the dissonant elements and resolve the seemingly different messages."[36] Even though we know these images are staged and choreographed, we cannot help but absorb the montage of images from the events.

Media Events Are Emotional

In a telling memo to President Carter before the 1980 campaign, Jerry Rafshoon comes to a conclusion that most presidential communication and media advisors have arrived at after experiencing America's mediated democracy:

> After a year in residence here I have come to one overriding and not very startling conclusion: In politics—or at least 1980 presidential politics—style is everything. Don't misunderstand. I want you to be President for another four years because I believe in what you're try-ing to do. But whether or not you are President for another four years does not depend so much on what you do between now and the elec-tion as how you do it.[37]

"Style is everything," Rafshoon argues. And while it is likely Rafshoon's ex-treme conclusion is based at least in part in his attempt to persuade a presi-dent diametrically opposed to all image-making attempts, his argument does stand up to scrutiny. In the modern rhetorical presidency, style is at least equal to substance, the visual is at least equal to the spoken, and the emo-tional is at least equal to the rational. Another impact of media events lies in their ability to tap into values and emotions in the audience and provoke an emotional response.

As described in the previous chapters, media events are often used in polit-ical contexts to tap into iconic, societal symbols and draw on the emotional power associated with those symbols. For example, candidates frequently sur-round themselves with American flags to take advantage of the flag's patriotic, historical, and mythic symbolism. American flags are ever present and ubiqui-tous at campaign events and in political advertisements. Candidates will go to great lengths to be photographed with the American flag—John Kerry hung an oversized flag on the ceiling and George H. W. Bush held a media event at a flag factory. Flags are not the only patriotic visual used by candidates; American presidents rarely miss an opportunity to speak at Mount Rushmore, the Statue of Liberty, or the Tomb of the Unknown Soldier.

Another type of societal symbol used by candidates in media events is the military and military personnel. Images of candidates with troops or military equipment are widespread, especially during war time. Politicians will commonly visit injured troops, don military uniforms, and tour weapons production facilities. Images from these media events tap into the emotions audiences have for troops and communicate the leader's strength and commitment to national defense.

A third common societal symbol commonly communicated through media events is the candidate playing or attending sports—especially sports central to the American experience. Candidates regularly stage events that feature themselves swinging a baseball bat or tossing around a football. Reagan went so far as installing a little league field on the White House lawn. Many candidates attend sporting events and participate in game rituals such as throwing out the first pitch of a baseball game. After the September 11 terrorist attacks, George W. Bush threw out the first pitch at Yankee Stadium at the first post-9/11 baseball game—simultaneously drawing on the emotions associated with baseball and the New York Yankees, America's team. Images from this event were prominently featured at the 2004 Republican National Convention just before Bush's convention address.

Media Events Influence Voters

Assessing the influence of media events on public opinion and voting behavior is difficult because a single event is not likely to significantly impact voters. Media events do not have a hypodermic effect on voters; instead the effects are indirect and cumulative. Events succeed because they disseminate hundreds of heuristic cues through the media space to voters. Any attempts to measure the effectiveness of appearances on public opinion are going be challenging methodologically because operationalizing such small and peripheral effects on voters is difficult.

The limited research that has been conducted has found that media events exert small but significant influence on public opinion and voting behavior. In one of the first analyses of presidential candidate appearances and public opinion, Daron Shaw concluded that three events in a state are worth approximately 1 percentage point of approval in public opinion polls.[38] In his groundbreaking book, Shaw expanded this research design to the 2000 and 2004 campaigns by comparing public events held by the candidates to the candidate's public opinion rating from daily tracking polls measured at both the state and media market level. Through this analysis Shaw was able to empirically conclude that holding a media event in a state or region increased the candidates' approval scores in small but important ways. Specifically, after holding all other factors constant, media events by Al Gore in 2000 increased his support by almost half a percentage point at the state level and 1.5 points at the media market level. An appearance by Joe Lieberman in a media market bumped up Gore's support numbers 1.9 points. In 2004, a visit from John Kerry resulted in an increase of .63 points in a media market and a visit from Edwards was associated with a .14 point bump. The numbers were positive for the Republican candidates in 2000 and 2004, but not as noteworthy. An appearance by Bush increased his vote share .26 points in a media market in 2000 and .96 points in 2004. A visit from Cheney improved Bush's numbers by .62 points in 2000 and 1.28 points in 2004. In each of these instances, the effect of appearances on candidate support was greater than television advertising effects in those same media markets. Dollar for dollar, media events were more impactful than television. For both Republicans and Democrats, Shaw's data shows that opinion change was always greater in a television media market than in the state as a whole, suggesting that the key to attitude change is exposure to the events on television.

What about voting behavior—do media events change the voting patterns and election outcomes? Althaus, Nardulli, and Shaw found that candidate appearances have a statistically significant effect on voting behavior, but those effects are usually small and tend to be counteracted by the compensatory campaign appearances and ads of the opposition candidate.[39]

In the same study described earlier, Shaw also looked at the relationship between media events and voting on Election Day. Shaw showed that "a four appearance swing through a battleground state would have netted an improvement ranging from 1 to 4 points in the candidate's relative favorability rating . . . [which] would have been worth about an extra point at the polls."[40] Putting it simply, in recent presidential elections, four events in a state would have persuaded one percent of voters to support your campaign. Shaw's research demonstrates that holding media events is correlated with increases in favorability toward the candidates and vote choice.

We should be cautious about over-emphasizing this research and should temper any arguments based on a single study, however, this pioneering research suggests that media events produce small but important effects—that media events matter.[41] As Shaw clarifies: "candidate activities affected candidate support in the predicted direction, but the effect tended to be on the order of tenths of percentage points. Thus building truly significant campaign effects required sustained weekly advantages or overwhelming advantages in a single week."[42] Media events have the potential to mobilize and persuade voters, they may not always do so, but often they do, especially when repeating similar themes. While these outcomes may be small and not necessarily determinative, they are important in battleground states that are often decided by small margins. In election years such as 2004, when eleven states had margins of victory less than 5 percentage points and twenty-one states had margins of less than ten, these small effects may prove to be decisive.

Conclusion

Media events have a significant and important influence on political campaigns and political communication in general; however, these effects are indirect and often epiphenomenal. As described throughout this chapter, the persuasive power of media events is their ability to set the media agenda, frame issues, and construct candidate images for voters. The unique communicative properties of events allow them to use emotion and drama to communicate across multiple channels using verbal and linguistic arguments. These indirect effects may also have main effects on voters; preliminary research by Shaw and his colleagues have uncovered direct effects of media events on public opinion and voting behavior.

Notes

1. Cited in Jessica Taylor, "From Watergate to Abu Ghraib Prison Scandal, CBS; Lesley Stahl Has Seen It All," *Furman University Office of News and Media Relations* (May 18, 2004), http://www.furman.edu/press/pressarchive.cfm?id=1957.

2. Jay Rosen, "Nobody Heard What You Said: Lesley Stahl's Fable about Reagan and the Press," *PRESSthink* (June 9, 2004), http://journalism.nyu.edu/pubzone/weblogs/pressthink/2004/06/09/Reagan_words.html, 1.

3. See Lesley Stahl, "The Press and the President," in *The Landon Lecture Series on Public Issues: The First Twenty Years, 1966–1986,* ed. Diana Carlin and Meredith A. Moore (Lanham, MD: University Press of America, 1990), 761–72; Lesley Stahl, *Reporting Live* (New York: Simon & Schuster, 1999); Taylor, "From Watergate."

4. For example, Keith Boykin, "The Politically Incorrect Guide to the Candidates," *KeithBoykin.com* (September 4, 2003), http://www.keithboykin.com/arch/2003/09/04/the_politically; David S. Broder, *Behind the Front Page: A Candid Look at How News is Made* (New York: Simon and Schuster, 1987); Glenn Elert, "Television and the Presidency: How the News Affects our Perceptions. *Hypertextbook.com* (March 24, 1992), http://hypertextbook.com/eworld/president.shtml; Rosen, "Nobody Heard"; Martin Schram, *The Great American Video Game: Presidential Politics in the Television Age* (New York: William Morrow, 1987).

5. Stahl, *Reporting Live,* 209–10.

6. Stahl, *Reporting Live*, 210.

7. Stahl, *Reporting Live*, 211.

8. Stahl, *Reporting Live*, 211.

9. Cited in Broder, *Behind the Front*, 181–82.

10. Rosen, "Nobody Heard."

11. Elert, "Television and the Presidency," 5.

12. Boykin, "The Politically Incorrect," 1.

13. Rosen, "Nobody Heard," 5–6.

14. Ronald Berkman and Laura W. Kitch, *Politics in the Media Age* (New York: McGraw Hill, 1986), 204–5.

15. Vernon F. Anderson and Roger Van Winkle, *In the Arena: The Care and Feeding of American Politics* (New York: Harper & Row, 1976), 352.

16. Memo, Rafshoon to Carter, 14 June 1977, folder: Image, box 34B, Office Files of Chief of Staff (Jordan), Carter Library.

17. Memo, Schneiders to Rafshoon, 10 July 1979, folder: Memoranda from Jerry Rafshoon–June, July, and August, 1979, box 28, Office Files of Greg Schneider, Carter Library.

18. Story of the Lady Bird Special, folder: Mrs. Johnson, box 2, WHCF: Trips 7-1-68, LBJ Library.

19. Anne Marie Barry, *Visual Intelligence: Perception, Image, and Manipulation in Visual Communication* (Albany: State University of New York Press, 1997); Doris A. Graber, *Processing Politics: Learning from Television in the Internet Age* (Chicago: The University of Chicago Press, 2001); Paul Messaris, *Visual Persuasion: The Role of Images in Advertising* (Thousand Oaks, CA: Sage, 1997).

20. Doris A. Graber, "Dissecting the Audio-Visual Language of Political Television," *Research in Micropolitics* 5 (1996a): 3–31, 12–13.

21. David Shaw, "News Often Has to Be Seen Before It Is Heard," *Los Angeles Times* (October 26, 1992), A16.

22. Kenny Irby, "When Seeing Is No Longer Believing: Photographers and Photo Editors Have the Obligation of Accuracy," *Nieman Reports* 58(1) (2004): 42.

23. Patrick S. Halley, *On the Road with Hillary: A Behind-the-Scenes Look at the Journey from Arkansas to the U.S. Senate* (New York: Viking, 2002), 19.

24. Daniel M. Shea and Michael John Burton, *Campaign Craft: The Strategies, Tactics, and Art of Political Campaign Management* (Westport, CT: Praeger Publishers, 2001).

25. Mary Anne Moffit, *Campaign Strategies and Message Design: A Practitioner's Guide from Start to Finish* (Westport, CT: Praeger Publishers, 1999).

26. Donald T. Regan, *For the Record: From Wall Street to Washington* (San Diego, CA: Harcourt Brace Jovanocich, 1988), 248.

27. For example, Raymond D. Strother, "Preparing Candidates for Television," in *The Manship School Guide to Political Communication*, ed. David D. Perlmutter (Baton Rouge: Louisiana State University Press, 1999), 176–85.

28. Susan Hendrix, "Planning Your TV Ads: The Pre-Production Process," *Campaigns and Elections* (September, 2001), 44–46, 45.

29. Strother, "Preparing Candidates," 179.

30. Michael K. Deaver and Mickey Herskowitz, *Behind the Scenes: In which the Author Talks about Ronald and Nancy Reagan . . . and Himself* (New York: Morrow, 1987), 141.

31. Memo, Parker to Haig, 11 February 1973, folder: Schedule Guidance, box 2, WHSF: O'Donnell, Nixon Presidential Materials.

32. Robert Schmuhl, *Statecraft and Stagecraft: American Political Life in the Age of Personality* (Notre Dame, IN: University of Notre Dame Press, 1990), 34.

33. Deaver and Herskowitz, *Behind the Scenes*, 140.

34. Jeff Zeleny, "Working Together, Obama and Clinton Try to Show Unity," *New York Times* (June 28, 2008).

35. Messaris, *Visual Persuasion*.

36. Schmuhl, *Stagecraft*, 32.

37. Memo, Rafshoon to Carter, folder: Memoranda from Jerry Rafshoon–June, July, and August, 1979, box 28, Office Files of Greg Schneider, Carter Library.

38. Daron R. Shaw, "A Study of Presidential Campaign Event Effects from 1952 to 1992," *Journal of Politics* 61(4) (1999): 893–913.

39. Scott L. Althaus, Peter F. Nardulli, and Daron R. Shaw, "Candidate Appearances in Presidential Elections, 1972–2000," *Political Communication* 19 (2002): 49–72.

40. Daron R. Shaw, *The Race to 270: The Electoral College and the Campaign Strategies of 2000 and 2004* (Chicago: The University of Chicago Press, 2006), 136.

41. Thomas M. Holbrook, *Do Campaigns Matter?* (Thousand Oaks, CA: Sage, 1996).

42. Shaw, *Race to 270*, 134.

CHAPTER 5

Implications for Communicating by Media Event

The purpose of this book was to cast a critical lens on media events and advance consultants to better understand how these events function rhetorically and the strategy and tactics used to execute these staged appearances. This book found that staging and managing media events is a daily concern for both candidates and elected officials and that major newsmakers almost never appear without the choreographic assistance of their advance staff. At once, both fascinating and frightening, candidates and elected officials now not only campaign by media event; they often govern via media event. It would not be a stretch to argue that we have moved to a "media event presidency." To carry out these performances, White House advancemen and -women and campaign media consultants have developed and perfected a sophisticated set of tools visually *write* events. This analysis has so far focused on describing and exploring these tools and their effects, this final chapter considers the lingering question of the normative consequences and implications of communicating through media events.

Scholars have been quick to attack the role of media events and visual symbols in politics and the academic literature is replete with examples of critics lambasting the current state of political and presidential rhetoric. The "rhetorical presidency," according to Jeffrey Tulis, has brought about "an erosion of the processes of deliberation, and a decay of political discourse."[1] Elvin Lim asserts that the current "anti-intellectual presidency" relies on simple platitudes and that current presidential speechmaking is "mere rhetoric" which "has created a pathology of vacuous rhetoric and imagery that has impoverished our public deliberative sphere."[2] And Bruce Miroff similarly argues that these "presidential spectacles" endorse "gesture over accomplishment and appearance over fact."[3] For George Edwards, "All a president can do is rely on rhetoric and symbols to obscure perceptions enough to be all things to all people."[4] Kenneth Burke noted the dulling effect politics has on speech, writing that political language functions to "sharpen up the pointless and blunt the too sharply pointed."[5] These arguments and the conclusions presented in this book raise the question: Are media events and advance good or bad for political discourse and the public sphere? Like most questions in political communication, the answer is complicated and depends on how candidates actually use this communication strategy and how journalists report on these events.

Staged events have become important political institutions. This is true for large events such as the party nominating conventions, but also applies to foreign trips, town halls, staged speeches, and campaign events. Just as candidate debates invite candidates to "enact the presidency,"[6] media events have an institutional function because they require candidates to rhetorically perform the role of president. And since communicating through media events is a fundamental duty of the presidency, events preview the communicative and leadership style of candidates and foreshadow presidential strengths and weaknesses. Voters can learn a great deal from staged events, and the best events inform and educate. Describing the purpose of government, Franklin Roosevelt underscored the role of communication in leadership: "Government includes the art of formulating policy and using political technique to attain so much of that policy as will receive general support; persuading, leading, sacrificing, teaching always, because the greatest duty of a statesman is to educate."[7] The statesman's duties described by Roosevelt can be accomplished through events. Media events excel at demonstrating, showing, explaining, and clarifying, and when used ethically reveal more than they conceal. Political leadership, especially presidential leadership, depends on effective communication, and staging media events are a central element of that communication. To diminish the importance of advance and media events as empty stagecraft or style over substance is overly simplistic and, in the end, wrong. This viewpoint incorrectly assumes that style and substance are separate and mutually exclusive, when in fact they are dependent upon each other in our mediated democracy. Substance without style will not be heard and is ineffective; style without substance is meaningless and obviously artificial. Style and substance—staging events and the events themselves—are inextricably connected and cannot be detached. In a political environment that is increasingly segmented and targeted with audience-specific messages, media events are one opportunity for true national messages which are broadcast to large audiences no matter the demographic or lifestyle classification.

It is understandable that newsmakers use media events—they allow them near absolute control of their message and allow candidates to say what they want to say, look how they want to look, and present their image of choice to the voter. Put simply, politicians continue to return to the media event technique because it works—it allows them to manage the media and present a favorable image to voters. But what is good for the politician is not necessarily good for public deliberation—a tension exists between the strength of media events to communicate a message and the weakness to potentially limit public debate. For example, when George W. Bush delivered a speech on the economy surrounded by packing boxes in a warehouse in St. Louis, Missouri, his advance staff covered the "Made in China" labels on each box and printed "Made in U.S.A." on the boxes pictured on the backdrop—literally covering up the message sent by the "off message" boxes. It is true that media events, like other types of persuasive communication, have the potential to short circuit public deliberation and political campaigns often strategically use events for this purpose. Since media events are equally equipped to generate heuristic cues as they are direct rational arguments, newsmakers may chose obfuscation over illumination. However, media events are not inherently unethical. The media event tactic by itself is amoral—it can be used for good and bad motives. Media events and visual symbols have equal potential to clarify and explain as they do to obfuscate and conceal. In fact, because events communicate using multiple channels—spoken, visual, and visceral—they can communicate additional information more quickly and in a form that more audiences can understand that words alone.

One red herring convoluting this debate is the contention that media events and visual symbols lack the ability to argue and intrinsically short circuit public deliberation, a claim that is frequently repeated in the scholarly literature. Denton and Hahn contend that, "Electioneering politicians no longer try to covert through argumentation; rather, they attempt to say something we in the audience can identify with, to project an image by what they say, to communicate something about their personalities by the audiences they chose to address."[8] This is not an issue solely with media events, but of the rhetorical presidency in general. Tulis reasons that when the executive branch rhetorically sets the terms of the debate, public deliberation is limited: "the continual attempts to mobilize the public through the use of personal or charismatic power de-legitimize constitutional or normal authority."[9] These concerns are justified, but they should be tempered. Traditional rhetorical critics like the ones cited above tend to have a limited definition of argumentation emerging from Aristotle's logical syllogism. "Good" argument to these scholars is composed of detailed policy claims supported by thorough evidence and backing with clearly stated warrants and nuanced premises. However, this definition indiscriminately discounts all forms of visual reasoning and affective logic, and as described in the first chapter, most voters process political information through these domains instead of through critical analysis and reflection. To borrow the language of Aristotle, visuals make enthymematic arguments—without explicit evidence, reasoning, or conclusions—but they are arguments none the less. As shown in this book, media events do make arguments and it is possible to deliberate via media event. Can visuals impede deliberation? Of course they can. Can we reason and debate via visuals? Yes, this is equally true. Ronald Reagan, perhaps the most successful of all visual presidents, frequently used visuals to improve the strength of his argument, as Wills observed, "(Reagan) is making a public argument, not merely a grand appearance. This is not just a matter of window dressing, but of constant analysis and testing of people's reactions. He is selling substance, not appearance—just as the advertiser is selling the product, not the slogan."[10]

Instead of diverting our attention to asking if visuals have a place in our public debate, we should accept that visual argumentation is here to stay and instead focus on developing a set of tools to analyze and evaluate these symbols. Because many of those visual images are enthymematic, visual arguments are more difficult to verify and substantiate. In lieu of logical operators and if-then statements, visuals symbols typically argue through association and disassociation.[11] As noted communication scholar Kathleen Hall Jamieson identifies, the visual properties of television allow politicians to "use (it) to short circuit the audience's demand that . . . claims . . . be dignified with evidence."[12] Beyond this enthymematic lack of evidence, visual symbols not only make arguments, they also frame issues. This visual framing can be subtle and may obfuscate damaging information from viewers. Messaris and Abraham argue that "viewers may be less aware of the process of framing when it occurs visually than when it takes place through words. Consequently, visual images may have the capacity of conveying messages that would meet with greater resistance if put in words, but which are received more readily in visual form."[13] Once again, this potential for deception is not unique to visual arguments or media events, but is nonetheless an area which should be noted. For these reasons, it is imperative that media events and the visual arguments they produce be further understood and scrutinized.

Much of the blame for the negative aspects of media events lies at the feet of journalists and the voting public. Operationally, candidates are required to use staged events to appeal to media outlets that focus on drama, personality, and the interesting visual image in their coverage, and the abundance of media events is largely a response to an electorate that is often disengaged and disinterested in politics. Put simply, if politicians did not stage events, they would lose elections and quickly fade from public memory. And while some commentators may decry the staging of politics, both the media and the public now expect professionally created and managed events. The ability to run a campaign and hold effective events is seen as a proxy for voter support and the ability to run an administration. When an event is not advanced and does not have the polish of a seasoned advance team, voters and media observers are much less likely to say, "wow, that was an authentic event" and much more likely to come away saying, "if they can't pull off a simple rally, how will they lead the country?" Advancing and carefully scripting events has become an ingrained part of contemporary political communication in American and is now required of major candidates by both journalists and voters.

In the television age, politicians who understand news management techniques are able to use the news media to their advantage. This book has documented that when in comes to media events, the political press is often happy to cover the events as staged at the benefit to the politician. More often than not, candidates and their advance staffs are able to use the strategies and tactics of media events to convert the media into reluctant allies. Even though the news media has the freedom to cover events in the manner they chose, the staging of events and the physical and symbolic control exerted by advance people have an effect on reporters. Too often, the press is more concerned about being fair to the politician, and is not diligent in asking if they are being fair to the public. In presidential campaigns, the focus is usually on the day-to-day grind of the campaign—who is ahead and who is behind in the polls and who said what at which event—and reporters almost never step back for perspective and context.

There is a complicated relationship between newsmakers and the journalists that cover their activities. Seib reviews this relationship: "The journalists try to gather information, the politicians try to shape the news. This process tends to become a struggle for control over the flow of information. Reporters can gather plenty of newsworthy material on their own, but they also need some cooperation from the candidates and staff members. Any major campaign will offer a rich diet of media events, but real news is often in short supply."[14] While the relationship can be adversarial, it is largely symbiotic—what is good for the candidate is usually also what is good for the reporter. Both campaigns and the news media want a compelling narrative, compelling pictures, and large audiences. Spending day after day with the subjects they are covering on the beat and on the trail, it becomes easy for the newswriter to be taken in by the newsmaker, especially because their fates are connected because the reporters assigned to cover presidential candidates on the trail expect to follow the victor to the White House beat. Reporters rarely deviate from the news narrative that has been established. Especially at the presidential level, politicians can control the rules of engagement and can "freeze out" reporters who do not follow those rules. According to Cook, "Reporters, dependent on presidents' cooperation, end up prisoners in the all but hermetically sealed pressroom, reluctant to roam far from their connection to fame and fortune in the news business. Instead of encouraging innovation and enterprise, the White House breeds concern among reporters about missing out on the story everyone else is chasing."[15] Members of the news media should recognize this relationship and understand the factors that allow newsmakers to exploit this relationship, control the news agenda, and receive favorable coverage.

Where reporters once criticized and rejected media events, they now accept them as part of the political communication process. Today, these manipulative techniques are so commonplace that they seldom receive mention. In his account of the "Boys on the Bus" in the 1972 presidential campaign, Timothy Crouse reported that "the term 'media event' had entered the language, and become a dirty phrase."[16] Crouse continued: "Many newspapermen complained that they would soon be relegated to the role of drama critics; they would merely write reviews of the spectacles staged for the benefit of TV crews. The TV people were extremely sensitive to all of this hostility, and even they were growing slightly resentful of media events."[17] Over 20 years later, after the 2004 campaign, the system that Crouse lamented has become widespread and his predictions have been validated. Alexandra Pelosi, who covered both the 2000 and 2004 campaigns explained:

> The minute you get assigned to cover a campaign, you become part of the process, a pawn in the campaign game. The news organizations hand their young over to the campaigns and let the Karl Roves of this world have their way with them. . . . You're stuck in this dysfunctional relationship between the news organization that has you there to do their bidding and the campaign who is trying to co-opt you. Over time, the relationship gets complicated, and you realize the dirty extent to which corporate media is in bed with the candidates.[18]

In her documentary on the 2000 Bush campaign, Pelosi described the day-to-day newsmaking process on the campaign trail: "Every day is a repeat of the day before. Bush feeds us the message of the day, the reporters file their stories, the TV producers feed their sound bites, we all feed ourselves, and then we're off to another event, where he gives the same stump speech again."[19] Pelosi is not alone in her analysis; many other journalists agree that the news media has been reduced to amplifiers for candidate's message. R. G. Ratcliffe, the political reporter for the *Houston Chronicle*, echoes, "I, like the rest of the press, we're all lemmings, we just follow this like little lemmings and do exactly what they say."[20]

So how are journalists to respond? They are at an impasse in which exposing advance efforts is both difficult and not rewarded; however, journalistic principles dictate they cover and broadcast details of the event. The Society of Professional Journalists' Code of Ethics directs journalists to further "public enlightenment . . . by seeking truth and providing a fair and comprehensive account of events and issues,"[21] however, in their coverage of media events many journalists reduce themselves to stenographers at best and flacks at worst. The detached and basic, "just the facts" style, reporting in which journalists focus on basics such as who, when, and where tilts the balance in favor of the political event stagers, and discounts the more central "why" questions which would help voters understand the day's events. Interpretation, analysis, context, and explanation must come with these facts, not after them, so voters can follow such staged events with added perspective and depth. As a 2008 research study funded by the Associated Press found, Americans are inundated with facts and breaking headlines through a variety of media, but they get very little back story and seldom dig deeper than the basic facts.[22]

It is important to remember that informing the public is the central goal of journalists. It is the job of reporters to call out candidates who conceal and deceive through media events and to inform voters about the work of advancemen and -women how they staged events. Journalists must hold public officials accountable and follow up descriptions of scripted events with explanations of how and why an event was constructed. Instead of relying on the journalistic crutch, "critics say," reporters should write with authority and make plain the handiwork of advance staffs. A short piece by Beth Fouhy for the Associated Press about a Hillary Clinton issue event serves as a model for how responsible journalists can cover heavily scripted events in a more transparent manner:

> Hillary Rodham Clinton, a former first lady who hasn't driven a car or pumped gas in many years because of Secret Service restrictions, joined a blue-collar worker at a filling station Wednesday to illustrate how the high price of gasoline is squeezing consumers.
>
> The Democratic presidential candidate and sheet metal worker Jason Wilfing, 33, pulled into the station in a large white Ford 250 pickup truck, Clinton riding shotgun. Never mind that it wasn't even Wilfing's truck, he had borrowed his boss's larger vehicle to accommodate Clinton's security agent and personal assistant, who rode in the back.
>
> Trailing Wilfing and Clinton was a Secret Service motorcade consisting of six gas-guzzling Suburbans, two squad cars and a green SUV bearing photographers and TV cameras. Several other reporters and cameramen stood shivering in unseasonably cold temperatures, ready to capture the multi-vehicle arrival.
>
> Clinton and Wilfing stepped out of the car and approached the pump. Wilfing chose regular unleaded gasoline, and began filling the tank. The two engaged in chit chat, with New York senator mentioning her proposal for a temporary gas tax holiday to ease the price pinch on consumers.
>
> The tank filled, Clinton looked at the price recorded at the pump and shook her head.
>
> "Sixty-three dollars," she said. "For just about half a tank."
>
> Shutters clicked, cameras whirred. Point made.[23]

In this story, Fouhy reveals the inconsistencies embedded in the event and correctly places the photo-op in an illuminating context for voters. While some may label this style of reporting as biased and lacking objectivity, the only prejudice in the story is to the true facts of the event and to readers. This type of story fulfills the journalist's code of ethics because it strives "to serve the public with thoroughness and honesty."[24] As Lesley Stahl learned in her attempts to critique the stage management of Reagan, reporters must always be aware of and consider limiting the artificial images of the events they broadcast because of the power of those images to connect and resonate with voters.

In is unclear how media convergence and new media technologies will impact advance efforts; however, three recent changes deserve mention. First, the advances of Internet video and video websites such as YouTube have shifted the visual imperative of television to news presented on the Internet. Increasingly, visuals are required for web content, which is likely to advantage political event planners. These sites have also turned the "gotcha journalism" of recent political coverage to a spectator sport. Now every second from every event is recorded, edited, and almost immediately uploaded to the Internet. What may have once been an off-the-record conversation with supporters now has an international audience in which a small slip of the tongue can end your political career, as George Allen discovered with his "Macaca" gaffe. This development has further institutionalized heavily scripted events because most candidates do not want to take a risk and speak extemporaneously. Second, with its explosion of news websites and blogs, the Internet has increased the size of the "news hole" journalists must fill each day. Most journalists, in addition to their regular duties, must also post blog entries throughout the day and they must do so quickly to be the first website with a story to generate web links and traffic. While this does afford journalists an opportunity to analyze and contextualize scripted events in a more personal context, such thoughtful criticism is difficult under deadline pressure. The norms that have emerged for online journalism privilege the new, brief, and interesting over the detailed and nuanced; which are likely to further entrench the media event tactic into political affairs. Third, the ubiquity of media has changed the way Americans consume the news. Instead of reading a daily newspaper or sitting down for the network evening news, more and more Americans use the Internet, e-mail, and other fast delivery outlets for quick-scan consumption.[25] This further decreases the demand for in-depth news coverage and makes it easier for politicians to only worry about the large headline and the powerful picture, given that most Americans won't care, read below the fold, or watch beyond the bottom-of-the-screen ticker.

The ultimate responsibility lies with the audience—the citizens whom the politician represents—to assess the messages and come to their own decisions about the appropriateness of a leader's media events. It is up to each of us to evaluate the media events we receive and the connections we make. To be better consumers of political messages, it would benefit citizens to understand the techniques and functions of media events—how the events are created and for what political purposes. This book is a step in that direction. By pulling back the proverbial curtain and revealing the advance "wizards" behind the curtain staging the events and the journalists behind the camera enabling the spectacles, citizens are better enabled to make informed decisions about which candidates to support and media outlets to watch and read. Politicians and the political media are practical beasts—they use and report on choreographed appearances because they work and as soon as voters react negatively and the politicians see the events as a failed strategy, they will shift to a new and more effective approach. If citizens are frustrated with the current scripted political events, they must voice their displeasure and demonstrate it in the voting booth. Political communication scholars must also play an increased role in educating the public and critiquing media events.

Implications for Political Communication Scholars

This study establishes that contemporary televised media events, in their entirety, are one of the primary communication techniques in political communication—both in electoral campaigns and also the governing and public debate process. Yet despite their importance, scholars lack a comprehensive understanding of how media events function: how they are created, covered by the news media, and received by audiences. The research and analysis presented here sets the foundation for the development of a model of media events.

The unique symbolic properties of a media event make it a distinct communicative form. Media events combine traditional notions of speechwriting, argumentation, and rhetoric with mythic symbols, visual communication, media management, staging, and advance. The multi-channelled nature of media events necessitates that scholars move beyond the text of a single speech on a single occasion and analyze a variety of texts using a variety of methods. A media event is more than a sum of its parts—it is a separate form with distant symbolic properties—so a distinct analytic framework is necessary to explain it rhetorical power. More research is needed to fully understand the complexity of media events. Rhetorical theory, political image theory, visual communication theory, and news management theory provide a solid theoretical foundation from which to build a media event analytic model which can be used to analyze and critique events. This model should examine four areas: (1) how an event's creation affects its rhetorical purpose, (2) the functions of visual and linguistic symbols in the event itself, (3) the role the media played in co-constructing the meaning of the event, and (4) the factors in the audience which may influence how an event was received.

The first element of an event which should be studied is the preparatory work done by the advance staff. Just as a public address scholar may include drafts of the text in their analysis, a critique of a media event must look at the strategy memos and diagrams of the visual speechwriters because there is great insight in studying the advance and the media events processes. Thus, scholars should not limit their analyses to the final event, but should also consider how events were created and the logic behind events. Multiple methods and multiple data sources allow scholars additional explanatory power through triangulation. Studying primary source material available in presidential libraries and through interviews with advance staff ground our understanding in first-hand accounts, which can uncover the motives, strategy, purpose, and development of the event. Doing so, when the materials are available, allows scholars to develop a more nuanced understanding and a richer perspective on the final product and its ultimate impact.

Second, scholars should also build on rhetorical theory to analyze the symbols in the media events themselves. This must be done holistically and not only focus on the text of speeches but also include how the candidate looked and acted, the make-up and message communicated by the crowd, the impact of the setting and backdrop, and the other visual symbols. It is essential for presidential rhetoric scholars to examine political messages in context and see how all elements of an event interacted. The critic should ask, "What is the message or messages communicated by this event?" and if the various messages had a reinforcing or amplification effect.

Even more importantly and third, we must understand how the media filter functions and how the interactions among the newsmakers and gatekeepers influenced coverage of each event. Because, by definition, media events are mediated, it is necessary to understand the selection process which influenced which elements of the media event were covered and which were not. That is, what unique symbolic attributes of media events influence the media frames in the corresponding coverage? This can only be done through analysis of the coverage itself. Scholars must review television, radio, print, and Internet coverage of an event to appreciate the appearance through voters' eyes and ears. Key questions include: What images were shown? What was the media's narrative or frame of the event? And what heuristics were broadcast to voters?

The last element that should be analyzed is the audience response—from both the direct audience and mediated audiences—to determine what, if any, affect the event had on public opinion. Critics should compare the candidate and advance staff's goals to the symbols in the event itself to the media coverage to determine the effectiveness of the event in communicating the newsmaker's desired message. Each of the candidate's goals should be considered for each of the various audiences to evaluate the event's impact. Where available, public opinion surveys can be consulted and commentaries from media experts can also be included for analysis.

REAGAN AT NORMANDY: A SAMPLE APPLICATION OF THE MEDIA EVENT ANALYTIC FRAMEWORK

To demonstrate the utility and explanatory power of this approach, the following section considers each of these elements by examining President Ronald Reagan's media events during the 40th anniversary of D-Day in greater depth. As Lou Cannon, one of the preeminent Reagan biographers argued, "Reagan's performance in Normandy demonstrated the timing, dramatic sense and attention to detail for which the White House staff was famous during his presidency,"[26] and it is therefore a good case study of how scholars can critique media events.

Reagan's series of media events on June 6, 1984 (Reagan's event at Pointe du Hoc and tour of the Ranger Monument, his visit to the American Ceremony, the event at the Omaha Beach memorial, and other D-Day anniversary events) were significant because they allowed Reagan an opportunity to reinforce his image as the new patriot who was willing to confront communism, but sought peace over war. Reagan used this international trip to demonstrate his leadership abilities and shape his image both at home and abroad at a critical time in his presidency during the 1984 campaign. As Ken Duberstein, Reagan's White House chief of staff, argued, "Pointe du Hoc and Omaha Beach were Reagan's signature moments. . . . As president, Ronald Reagan delivered three unforgettable speeches: Pointe du Hoc, the Challenger disaster, and the Berlin-tear-down-this-wall number. But it was the first of these—Pointe du Hoc—that set the tone for the others."[27]

In April of 1984, National Security Advisor Robert McFarlane provided the president and his staff an outline of the European trip, complete with a daily schedule and suggested objectives for the trip. The first four days of Reagan's ten-day trip would be spent in Ireland, where Reagan would emphasize economic and cultural ties between the two countries through a series of policy speeches and public events. On Tuesday, April 5, Reagan would hold talks with Prime Minister Margaret Thatcher to demonstrate American-English unity before crossing the English Channel to France. In an early memo, the events were given one paragraph:

> *Wednesday, June 6. Visit to Normandy.* (Three sites: Pointe du Hoc, the American cemetery memorial and Utah Beach.) Normandy symbolizes

the US commitment to Europe, which led directly to the Atlantic Alliance. The President will make brief (10–15 minutes) remarks at the Pointe du Hoc ceremony to about 500 people, including veterans groups. This should be emotional, stirring, and personal. The themes include reconciliation of former adversaries, how postwar cooperation has kept the peace for the longest period in modern European history, Alliance solidarity, and the strength of the American commitment to Europe.[28]

This early strategy memo guided the speechwriters and advance personnel.

Peggy Noonan, who had recently been hired from CBS to write epideictic speeches such as eulogies and dinner toasts, was selected to write the Pointe du Hoc address. As a guide for her speech, Noonan researched Reagan's June 6, 1982 remarks for the 38th Anniversary of D-Day and received several memos from various foreign policy advisors within the administration.[29]

All of the events in this European trip were selected and managed to communicate specific objectives. Strategy choices were not limited to what the President would say; they also considered where the events would take place and the symbolic power of those settings. As a memo to the president described:

> The settings for the visits are colorful and dramatic. The return home to Ireland, the remembrance of Allied sacrifices forty years before in Normandy, and the historic splendor of London provide the President with an ideal backdrop for his themes of peace and prosperity and the importance of Allied support and cooperation in the achievement of both.[30]

It is clear from this early stage that Reagan's staff were concerned with putting the president in dramatic situations to grab media attention and in symbolic settings to bolster his image in addition to the words he would speak.

While Noonan was penning the speech, Deaver and Henkel went to Normandy and did the advance for the European trip. It was Henkel who traversed the nine miles of beach area scouting for and selecting the most dramatic location—Pointe du Hoc.[31] Henkel and Deaver knew the location was perfect because it had all the elements of a good event site: "Pointe du Hoc is a knife, stood on its edge, pointed into the sea. It looks lethal, a palisade of boulder and mean rocks where Normandy's green softness has reclaimed nothing."[32] The rocky crag emerging from the English Channel had a majestic natural beauty, remnants of bunkers remained for Reagan to tour, and veterans from the battle would be in the audience. Deaver knew the emotion of the event would translate on television:

> I was interested in the choreography of the event, making sure we had the right visuals. Remember, we had a fleet of ships off in the distance.

We used the coast as a backdrop. All the TV producers were sent stories of "the boys" in attendance in advance. As Reagan was saying
those words—if you look at the film—the camera was going to flash
on one or two of the Rangers. When Reagan acknowledged them, the
camera would flash to Reagan wiping away tears. It would be a powerful image.[33]

Deaver and Henkel also advanced the American cemetery in Normandy and the
Omaha Beach event location. Just as much, if not more, time, money, personnel, and resources were devoted to constructing and designing the event as were
spent crafting the words the president would deliver. The advance staff created
the event much as the speechwriter writes a speech.

The Omaha Beach speech was originally considered the important speech of
the day and was written by Tony Dolan. Looking for a dramatic hook, Dolan
read the letters from D-Day families that had been written to the president in
advance of the trip.[34] A letter from Lisa Zanatta Henn expressing her late father's
desire to return to Normandy grabbed Dolan because it felt real, and he integrated large sections of the letter into his manuscript.

Even though they were visitors on foreign soil, the White House staff
planned every moment of Reagan's schedule and did not leave any elements to
chance: the Pointe du Hoc veterans were in place, the news media had been
alerted to the importance of the event, and U.S. destroyers glided in the Channel off the beach as a backdrop. Reagan tried to create a sweeping sense of patriotism using basic American symbols such as the flag, the World War II generation, the cemetery in Normandy, and the cliffs of Pointe du Hoc. Crowds of
veterans were assembled to support Reagan, and the president stopped on his
mark and saluted the veterans on cue. The graves of fallen Americans at the Normandy cemetery allowed Reagan the opportunity to show he understood the sacrifice of those who fought in World War II and simultaneously tap into American's emotions for those soldiers.

Reagan's remarks at Pointe du Hoc served two explicit purposes—to honor
the soldiers that fought in World War II and to reiterate his "peace through
strength approach" to the Soviet Union. The first goal is accomplished in several moving passages in the first half of the speech. Reagan says, "These are the
boys of Pointe du Hoc. These are the men who took the cliffs. These are the
champions who helped free a continent. These are the heroes who helped end
a war."[35] These remarks had added power because of the setting of the event and
the context in which Reagan was speaking. The veterans in attendance were vis-
ibly emotional and several wept as Reagan spoke. Reagan's words were powerful, and the power of the battle site gave additional strength to Reagan's words.
After recounting the stories of several of the soldiers, Reagan stresses, "You all
knew that some things are worth dying for. One's country is worth dying for,

and democracy is worth dying for, because it's the most deeply honorable form of government ever devised by man. All of you loved liberty. All of you were willing to fight tyranny."[36] Reagan appealed to the core values of the American people, and the embodiment of those values—the veterans in attendance at the speech—reinforced those values and Reagan's words.

The second explicit goal of this address was to reiterate Reagan's commitment to peace with the Soviet Union, but only if they agreed to shared principles such democracy and freedom. Near the end of the speech, just as he recalled the sacrifice of Americans in World War II, he also remembers the losses of the Soviet Union:

> It is fitting to remember here the great losses also suffered by the Russian people during World War II: 20 million perished, a terrible price that testifies to all the world the necessity of ending war. I tell you from my heart that we in the Unites States do not want war. We want to wipe from the face of the Earth the terrible weapons that man now has in his hands. And I tell you we are ready to seize that beachhead. We look for some sign from the Soviet Union that they are willing to move forward, that they share our desire and love for peace, and that they will give up the ways of action.[37]

By embedding this appeal within an epideictic address, Reagan was able to frame the struggle against communism alongside the struggle against fascism in World War II. This allowed Reagan to not only restate the core values that he believed separated the United States from the Soviet Union, it gave Reagan the opportunity to argue that arms reduction and peace is the only acceptable solution. Again, the context of the speech magnified its significance.

There was an implied goal of Reagan's event that was present in both the words he spoke and the images that were generated in the event. The event was used to reinforce Reagan's presidential image and refute criticisms of the president for American voters. The events portrayed Reagan as a leader who was committed to the core values of the country, such as freedom, patriotism, and liberty. The events also refuted the common criticism that Reagan was a warmonger who would lead the country into a third World War. By both commemorating those who died in Normandy and reaching out to the Soviets, these events displayed Reagan as a patriot who understood that some wars are worth fighting, but peace is a preferred outcome.

In the events, Reagan tapped into the core values of America and personified the World War II generation. In the words of historian Douglas Brinkley,

> There was nothing boring, hokey, or mundane about his demeanor. When he saluted the flag it was done with such conviction that it

made you want to stand up straight yourself, to embrace the fact that you too were part of the great American pageant. He was the American statesman about to remind the American people—with the English Channel and Pointe du Hoc Ranger Monument at his back—what true patriotism was all about.[38]

Martin Schram argued that Reagan played the role of leader of the free world for all it was worth: "Reagan was there on the bluff overlooking the beach, fighting back tears, paying true tribute, with the blue of the sea behind him and the wind blowing just a bit, biting his lip and saying in a way that makes us all proud of our country and out president: 'These are the boys of Pointe du Hoc.'"[39] On D-Day, Reagan spent the day at an Army film studio, but on the 40th anniversary of D-Day he was giving a more commanding performance—both honoring and personifying what would later be called the greatest generation. Ronald Reagan was encouraging a New Patriotism in the country—and his desired image was of the ideal New Patriot.

Securing television coverage back home in the United States was a primary concern for Deaver and the advance staff. In the original schedule for June 6, French president Francois Mitterrand was to greet Reagan in a French-American ceremony at Omaha Beach scheduled to begin at 4:00 p.m., or 10:00 a.m. EDT, too late for the morning television news shows in the eastern United States.[40] Reagan's image makers pressed the French government to allow Reagan to speak before joining other allied leaders at Utah Beach for the formal anniversary ceremony. Because of this lobbying, Reagan's remarks were heard live on all three television networks by millions of Americans on the day after the final Democratic presidential primary of the year.

And the coverage that Reagan received was overwhelmingly positive—especially on television.[42] In the midst of the presidential campaign, Reagan received extensive and uncritical coverage of his events at Pointe du Hoc, Omaha Beach, and the Normandy cemetery. Photographs of him speaking at Pointe du Hoc, laying flowers at the Normandy cemetery, and saluting veterans ran in most newspapers around the country alongside the text of his remarks. On television, a poetic montage of shots created the image of a strong but temperate commander in chief; Reagan is shown talking with and saluting the Army Rangers, touring the remains of the battle sites, and breaking down as he read the letter from Zanetta. The visuals in the story closely resembled those in Reagan's "Morning in America" series of television advertisements, using rosy shots of Reagan surrounded by flags and veterans.

There was some mention of the manufactured nature of the events in both the print and television coverage of the events. NBC showed toe marks taped to the ground so the president would know where to stand for one of the photo-ops and NBC reporter Mary McGrory noted that "everything was stage-managed to the minute."[43] The CBS piece noted that a camera crew from the Republican National Committee was following Reagan to gather footage for the 1984 campaign. Of course, CBS did not acknowledge that their camera was also following Reagan, that they were shooting the same footage, and that their story itself looked and sounded like a political advertisement.

In summary, this analysis illustrates success of the image-building process perfected by the Reagan media events team. In Normandy, Reagan's staff united the president's remarks with patriotic American symbols, supportive crowds of veterans, and an emotionally powerful setting to build Reagan's "New Patriot" image just months before the election. Reagan's staff effectively used visual communication principles to surround the president with patriotic symbols, supportive crowds, and mediagenic backdrops. For the most part, the press accepted Reagan's events at face value and transmitted the favorable words, sounds, and pictures from the event into American homes—a free political advertisement on the nightly news. Of course, the event was anything but spontaneous, as Deaver, Noonan, Henckle, and the rest of the Reagan team planned and controlled nearly every symbolic element of the event in an attempt to build Reagan's image. This analysis supports the assertion by commentator Michael Barone that "In retrospect, the election was over by June 6."[44] Through these media events— and the visual and verbal symbols that constituted them—Reagan effectively constructed an image of the "New Patriot." This image was later supported by Reagan's "Morning in America" campaign, which prominently featured images from these events. Mondale found it difficult to challenge this image in 1984, and Reagan won in a landslide.

Notes

1. Jeffrey K. Tulis, *The Rhetorical Presidency* (Princeton, NJ: Princeton University Press, 1987), 176)

2. Elvin T. Lim, *The Anti-Intellectual Presidency: The Decline of Presidential Rhetoric from George Washington to George W. Bush.* (New York: Oxford University Pres, 2008), 4.

3. Bruce Miroff, "The Presidential Spectacle," in *The Presidency and the Political System*, ed. Michael Nelson (Washington, DC: CQ Press, 2003), 278–303, 302.

4. George C. Edwards, *The Public Presidency* (New York: St. Martin's, 1983), 199.

5. Kenneth Burke, *A Grammar of Motives* (New York: Prentice Hall, 1945), 393.

6. Edward A. Hinck, *Enacting the Presidency: Political Argument, Presidential Debates and Presidential Character* (Westport, CT: Praeger, 1993); Kathleen Hall Jamieson and David S. Birdsell, *Presidential Debate: The Challenges of Creating an Informed Electorate* (New York: Oxford University Press, 1988).

7. *The Public Papers of Franklin D. Roosevelt, 1928–1932,* "Campaign Address, Commonwealth Club, San Francisco," 9/23/1932.

8. Robert E. Denton, and Dan F. Hahn, *Presidential Communication: Description and Analysis* (New York: Praeger, 1986), 288.

9. Tulis, *Rhetorical Presidency,* 190.

10. Garry Wills, *Reagan's America: Innocents at Home* (Garden City, NY: Doubleday, 1987), 324.

11. Paul Messaris, *Visual Persuasion: The Role of Images in Advertising* (Thousand Oaks, CA: Sage, 1997).

12. Kathleen Hall Jamieson, *Eloquence in an Electronic Age: The Transformation of Political Speechmaking* (New York: Oxford University Press, 1988), 13.

13. Paul Messaris and Linus L. Abraham, "The Role of Images in Framing News Stories," in *Framing Public Life: Perspectives on Media and our Understanding of the Social World,* ed. Stephen D. Reese, Oscar H. Gandy, and August E. Grant (Mahwah, NJ: Lawrence Erlbaum Associates, 2001), 215–26, 225.

14. Philip M. Seib, *Who's in Charge?: How the Media Shape News and Politicians Win Votes.* Dallas: Taylor, 1987), 58–59.

15. Timothy E. Cook, *Governing with the News: The News Media as a Political Institution* (Chicago: University of Chicago Press, 1998), 134.

16. Timothy Crouse, *The Boys on the Bus* (New York: Random House, 1973), 139.

17. Crouse, *The Boys,* 139–40.

18. Alexandra Pelosi, *Sneaking into the Flying Circus: How the Media Turn our Presidential Campaigns into Freak Shows* (New York: Free Press, 2005), ix.

19. Alexandra Pelosi, George W. Bush. *Journeys with George: A Home Movie* [videorecording]. United States: HBO Video (2004).

20. Pelosi, *Journeys with George.*

21. Society of Professional Journalists. Code of Ethics. Available at http://www.spj.org/ethicscode.asp.

22. Associated Press, "A New Model for News: Studying the Deep Structure of Young-Adult News Consumption," A Research Report from the Associate Press and the Context-Based Research Group, *Associated Press* (June 2008). Available at http://www.ap.org/newmodel.pdf

23. Beth Fouhy, "Play of the Day: Clinton Visits Gas Station for Cameras," *Associated Press* (May 1, 2008).

24. SPJ Code of Ethics.

25. Associated Press, "New Model; The Pew Research Center for the People & the Press," *Associated Press* (August 17, 2008). Audience Segments in a Changing News Environment: Key News Audiences Now Blend Online and Traditional Sources. 2008 Pew Research Center Biennial News Consumption Survey.

26. Lou Cannon, "At 40th D-Day tribute, Reagan Took the Occasion by Storm," *Washington Post* (June 6, 2004), A6.

27. Quoted in Douglas Brinkley, *The Boys of Pointe du Hoc: Ronald Reagan, D-Day and the U.S. Army 2nd Ranger Battalion* (New York: William Morrow, 2005), 7.

28. Memo, Your Trip to Europe—Annotated Agenda, Reagan Library.

29. Brinkley, *The Boys of Pointe du Hoc,* (Noonan, 1990).

30. Memo, Your Trip to Europe—Annotated Agenda, Reagan Library.

31. Brinkley, *The Boys of Pointe du Hoc.*

32. John Vinocur, "D-Day + 40 Years," *New York Times* (May 13, 1984), 14.

33. Quoted in Brinkley, *The Boys of Pointe du Hoc,* 176

34. Brinkley, *The Boys of Pointe du Hoc.*

35. Remarks at a Ceremony Commemorating the 40th Anniversary of the Normandy Invasion, D-Day (1984, June 6). The Public Papers of President Ronald W. Reagan. Ronald Reagan Presidential Library. Available at http://www.reagan.utexas.edu/archives/speeches/1984/60684a.htm.

36. Remarks at a Ceremony, 2.

37. Remarks at a Ceremony, 3.

38. Brinkley, *The Boys of Pointe du Hoc,* 234–35.

39. Martin Schram, *The Great American Video Game: Presidential Politics in the Television Age* (New York: William Morrow, 1987), 63.

40. Lou Cannon, *President Reagan: The Role of a Lifetime* (New York: Public Affairs, 2000).

41. Cannon, *President Reagan.*

42. Tom Brokaw, Jim Bitterman, and Chris Wallace, "D-Day Anniversary," *NBC Evening News* (June 6, 1984). Available at http://tvnews.vanderbilt.edu; Sam Donaldson, "D-Day Anniversary," *ABC Evening News* (June 6, 1984). Available at http://tvnews.vanderbilt.edu; Dan Rather, Bill Plante, and Tom Fenton, "D-Day Anniversary," *CBS Evening News* (June 6, 1984). Available at http://tvnews.vanderbilt.edu.

43. Brokaw, Bitterman, and Wallace, "D-Day Anniversary."

44. Cited in Cannon, "At 40th D-Day," A6.

Index

About the Author

Dan Schill is an assistant professor of corporate communication and public affairs at Southern Methodist University, where he specializes in political communication, media and politics, and presidential rhetoric. His research and news analysis has been featured in news publications such as the *Wall Street Journal*, *Chicago Tribune*, and *Dallas Morning News*, as well as on CNN and ABC News.

CPSIA information can be obtained at www.ICGtesting.com
Printed in the USA
LVOW090932030712

288676LV00004B/89/P